Broken Unto Light!

"A story of love, pain and forgiveness"

JAMARRA MOTA

Copyright © 2024 Jamarra Mota
All rights reserved.
ISBN: 9798877680296

DEDICATION

I would like to dedicate this book to all the broken, hurting, and over-guarded women of the world. "Brokenness can lead to beauty, but it's how you respond through the journey on the way to light".

~Jamarra Mota~

ACKNOWLEDGEMENT

I would like to acknowledge my Abba father for inspiring me to create this book, as well as Michelle P Crump for being my dedicated and wonderful publisher.

Table of Content

Introduction 1

Chapter 1 – Intrigued at First Sight 2

Chapter 2 – The Lovely Coincidence 5

Chapter 3 – Friendship to Love 12

Chapter 4 – Playing With Fire 16

Chapter 5 – Crutch to Confession 29

Chapter 6 – Are You Ready? 36

Chapter 7 – Monster Moves 44

Chapter 8 – Obedience Is Better 82

Chapter 9 – No More Apologies 89

Chapter 10 - Finding Light: My Note to Women 95

Conclusion - Finding Light: My Note To Women 99

Author's Autobiograpy - Jamarra Mota 102

Introduction

Everyone must undergo the process of learning and growing. This process often includes gains, losses, trials, wins, and mistakes. Each person's life story has a unique ending - some may overcome challenges and survive, while others may remain stuck or succumb to their struggles. This story is about a beautiful young girl who did not recognize her worth. She fell in love, and experienced heartbreak, but eventually gained self-worth to later embark on a journey toward purpose. With this narrative, I'm hoping that you will walk away with encouragement and self-awareness.

My story is not different than many others, I'm quite sure, but what sets me apart from so many young girls is that I survived. No longer a victim but a victor. To be counted as such is a blessing. I pray that my testimony will inspire and uplift you in more ways than one. May it transform your mind and change the very trajectory of your life for the better. This is my truth. The hard truth of love, lies, deception, jealousy, hate, pain, bitterness, and most importantly, recovery. A story where purpose overturned what could have been a gruesome fate. However, before we get to the bulk of the journey, I would like to travel back and show you the beginning perceived through my eyes. In order to appreciate an outcome, one must see the process.

CHAPTER ONE

Intrigued at First Sight

It was a calm day at Excelsior Reed Highschool. I had just been dropped off by my neighbor Mr. D. An old man who was tired of my crap but loved me as a daughter, nonetheless. In the morning, I would usually go inside and find a good corner to get in and read just before the bell rings. However, this day was different. This was the first week of twelfth grade. I had just turned seventeen a couple of months prior to this day and was super excited about what senior year had to offer. As I was patiently waiting for my cousin Janeisha to arrive at school; so that we could walk in together, I was quickly taken aback. In the parking lot, my eyes stumbled across a beautiful young stranger.

This stranger's fair countenance, long hair, and striking eyes that were semi-slanted had caught my attention and had me inquiring. For a moment he was all I saw. For the moment this young man had stolen my focus and captivated my eyes. Before scolding myself from within, the usual tactics to help me gain concentration; another question surfaced instead. Who was he? Just in the nick of time, Janeisha arrived and pulled my attention back into focus or should I say perspective. Besides someone who looked like that would never notice someone like me, I thought to myself silently. During school hours it was the same old', same old'. Students, teachers, admin, business, and the not-so-important but important for the time, hall community. The hall community is everything that transpired throughout the transition to the next period.

There were the fashionistas who were running their mouths in the hall about the next set of shoes, and the hottest gossip. Then you had the groups of talkers but walkers (these were the students that did not stand around. They cared for conversation but communicated while walking so that they would be on time to class). Then you had the layers. Layers were the students that clung posted up on the walls; the students that didn't move until security spoke.

These students did not care about being late. On top of this hall community, you had very prepared students who took their education seriously. I always loved to do that. To look at someone and try to guess where they are in life at that moment. Finally, there was me. The one that wanted to do great in school, but never saw life past the first year of college. The girl who loved to read, took education seriously and genuinely loved people but tried to keep to herself for the most part. Avoiding all the scattered possible confusion and unnecessary drama. Very different from the teenage norm I suppose, but it worked. This is what worked for me. I had friends but there was no drama.

In the first period, I found a seat in the middle of the class. There was a lady who was temporarily there until the actual teacher placement arrived. "Hello, ladies and gentlemen." A woman with a very fair countenance and decent height walked in. This was the substitute teacher. On this day she educated us on the term malleable intelligence and how intelligence was not a fixed trait. I remembered this because this gave me a deep sense of hope for those students who believed they would never amount to nothing because of their parents.

I always hated it when people had a dead-end mindset when it came to learning. At least this was one of the hottest topics debated in journalism the prior year.

As I was drifting off down memory lane thinking of the arguments that I could have thrown on the table, a friend of mine struck up a conversation. Speaking in a tone that would keep us under the radar of being caught by the sub; we spoke on life. Before the end of that conversation, E.J. asked me something I did not expect. "Hey Jamarra, would you mind being my dance partner in my best friend's Quinceañera". I told him sure; I wouldn't mind; informing him that I would ask my mom and get back to him. Very surprised and thrilled at the offer; I did not fathom that this event would be the catalyst that changed my life.

CHAPTER TWO

The Lovely Coincidence

Saturday came, and there was not a cloud in the sky. I was waiting for E.J. to call to let me know when they were outside. Once the group reached, I grabbed up my belongings and bolted out the door. As I locked the door, I looked back at the nude van with excitement. I never was a part of a Quinceañera, and I was thrilled to be a participant in one. As I entered the van and spoke to everyone, something egged me to look back. Looking back, sent flutters through my stomach because a young man was laying his head on a young lady's lap. This wasn't just any young man. It was him. It was that lovely stranger that I saw in the parking lot that school morning.

It was that young man whom I couldn't get out of my mind since my eyes first took possession of his countenance. What a coincidence. Who would have known that this would be the day? The day that the young man I was thinking of would arrive directly on my doorstep. Who was this young man? Why was I thinking of him for an entire day? This was not like me. I mean I had a surplus of handsome young men around me prior to seeing him, but it wasn't a big deal before. Like no one ever fluttered my mind to that extent and capacity. For me, it would be oh snap, he is gorge and that would be the end of it. However, with him, this was not the case.

After these thoughts walked through my head, I pondered and stumbled across a brave idea. Let me introduce myself. After all, it would be a try. On her lap, he appeared to be asleep, but that made me no never mind. I smiled and poked him, nonetheless. For I had an idea. An idea of introducing myself accompanied with all my personality. An idea of stepping out of my shell to show my weird, goofy, spontaneous, and loving personality. So, I turned around and simply poked him in his side.

Once I poked him, he looked up in what one would guess to be amazement. I gently smiled and waved frantically. He put his head back down and went back to sleep. I turned back around and chuckled. During the practice, the entire group had a chance to get acquainted. We learned each other's names and some of each other's likes. I learned that his name was P.J. While being dropped home, one thing I thought the most about was how I couldn't wait till our next practice. After a few practices, it was time for the actual sweet fifteen.

The ladies who were dancers in the Quinceañera were required to meet at Izzie's house for makeup and dressing. Izzie's sister had made all of the ladies look exceptionally beautiful, including me. Would this be the night? Would he notice me? When we arrived at the hall and exited the limousine, a few of the young ladies and I were escorted in. The hall was so beautiful, with roses and gold trimmings. The colors of the hall were put together splendidly, and people were dressed so eloquently. I was in awe and sheer amazement. It was like something I had seen on TV, or in a wedding magazine.

Don't be mistaken, my mother always provided my siblings and I with the best of the best. I wasn't lacking anything. However, it was nice to see other cultures and the way that they jazzed up their events. It was nice to see and taste a part of me that was not displayed in my home. During the Quinceañera, I was having so much fun that the thought of him, time, and other wants, did not cross my mind; it wasn't till almost after the Quinceañera, that it dawned on me. Will this be the last time I dare to speak to this lovely stranger or even be this close? After the quince was over, I thought, this is it. This would be the last time, and then back to my everyday norm.

The normal tucking myself in a corner of the school and reading a good book to drown out the noise. I never really noticed how much I isolated myself until this major event. My freshman year was very different from that of the start of twelfth grade. Freshman year, I was much more fun, lively outspoken, crazy, and boisterous. During freshman year I had belt fights with seniors, joined a few clubs, and was in a dance group called Mass Destruction. At that time, I had so many school friends, but when the seniors graduated, I was able to see the high school environment for what it was. A vapor.

An experience that happens quickly and ends quickly. It was not that my peers were bad students, but it was easier to stay away and keep a closer circle. Therefore, from eleventh through twelfth grade that's how I mostly kept things. "When it was time to go home Izzie's sister asked P.J. to take several of the dancers home. "Wait a minute.

Someone who is a year younger than me is driving, what is this? I thought to myself". Not to mention, I just so happen to be one of the group members she asked P.J. to take home. Stop playing, is this safe? I continued." As I took a deep breath, I thought but wait a minute, I would like this. I would like another moment with him. Another moment to see who he was past his looks. I want to see who this person is. This person that acquired so much of my interest. Besides it's not like I was no scary cat either.

Out of the three siblings on my mother's side, I was the wildest and most rugged child she had. I loved nature, tree climbing, fighting my homeboys in the neighborhood, and the frequent basketball games we would have. Although that was my elementary and middle school years, it was still a part of me. I thought to myself if anything, he should be the one afraid, not me. After reminding myself of who I was, I got into his car. Having asked a few of the dancers whom he was not well acquainted with for their addresses, P.J. then asked with a calm voice, "Jamarra where do you live again"?

For a second, I looked at him speechless, took a deep breath, and then I gave him my address. I was trying not to be so nervous while speaking. That deep breath came in handy. "Oh, yes, he replied. "I know exactly where that is. You live on the west side of North Miami Avenue". As he was dropping everyone off, I couldn't help but think about the why's? and the how's? How is it possible for someone younger than me to already be driving, and know their direction around Miami?

Why wasn't I really driving yet? And what was I waiting for, the year of the rat? I mean I took driver's ed, but driving out in about, especially at night was not the case. I went everywhere on foot, took my landmarks, and made sure to be back in the house at a decent hour. How is it that this young man was capable of driving at an hour such as this? The time was a few minutes shy of 10pm. As. P.J. was driving he looked very focused, mature, and mysterious. I took this time to scan him thoroughly.

His eyebrows, eyes, lips, cheekbone, physique, and lastly his hands. His hands were so beautiful. Almost like someone had painted them on a canvas. His hands attracted me the most. Among being carefree, I was also very peculiar. It would be some of the weirdest things that attracted me to people. Things like someone's smell or laugh. After staring at him for a while, I realized that not only was I intrigued but I was now dangerously attracted to this young man. Although I did not truly know him apart from the few dance practices, I wanted more. P.J. drove everyone else home first. After the last dancer was dropped off, he looked over in the passenger seat at me and said, "Now it's your turn."

When we arrived at my house, instead of dropping me off, he parked the car, turned to me, and started asking a bunch of questions. I chuckled softly and said how about we go to a park near me to talk. "Very well" he replied and was obliged. Once arriving at the park, he and I began to speak with one another. We spoke about almost everything. Covering school, hobbies, and funny childhood moments.

P.J. wanted to know more about me, and I him. While we discussed some of our interests, he began venting about his mother and I then joined him. My mother and I had a disagreement the same day of the Quinceañera, so she refused to see me before I left. This made me a little disappointed, but I still went to the party and enjoyed myself, nevertheless. I found it strange how we both got into a disagreement with our moms on the same day. From this, I asked P.J. for his mother's name.

Reminding him of how we went on a thirty-minute rant about our mothers but never exchanged their names. P. J looked over with those semi-slanted eyes and said, "My mother's name is Janie". In a loud yelp, I threw my head back in great laughter. With a strong look of concern, P.J picked up his keys to turn the car on. I laughed even harder, grabbed his shoulder, and said relax. I'm not crazy it's just my mother's name is Janie as well. We both fell out in laughter as P.J. said that for a moment he assumed I was crazy, and he was going to quickly take me home. Hearing the word home, I looked at the time and said I had to go.

He brought me home as the perfect gentleman and we exchanged numbers. Every day after this P.J. and I spent time. I introduced him to my family and was able to meet his parents. His father and mother came over to meet my mother. His mother was very fair, and his father looked exotic. Ms. Janie had thick black hair twisted perfectly in a hair clip. She was so beautiful. Finding out more about P.J. made me happy. He was wild, crazy, and free just like me.

It made me feel like I finally found someone, someone that would understand. I did not put a name or pin to what this feeling was, but I knew one thing I was most certain about was that I never wanted it to end.

CHAPTER THREE

Friendship to Love

Slowly but surely as the days progressed, I did not want to be a minute without him. There were a lot of things I found in him to be exceptional. I appreciated his loyalty, and sincerity as a friend. P. J was born and raised a vegetarian (which was not something I too much cared for but respected), and he was adventurous and witty. This was something I loved. I loved our water fights, pillow fights, car games, and everything in between.

We would fall asleep over the phone together wake up and begin a new conversation. Hearing his voice in the morning was super cute to me. Where little by little we formed a bond, a soul tithe. Falling in love but titling it as best friendship. During our free time on the weekends, we would swim together. P.J. enjoyed swimming. Swimming always brought out conversation. While swimming we would converse and discuss every little thing. One of the times P.J. informed me of how I was so privileged to have such a beautiful house with a pool in the backyard.

He began telling me of some of his childhood occurrences that were not very polite. Some of the sufferings that he endured, that he wasn't looking for sympathy on, made me ponder. I pondered on the mere fact that if I had known him sooner, I could have helped him. My mom was quick to assist individuals in need, so I just knew we would have helped. A growing flutter arose in me that day. A few weeks after this, I finally went to spend time with him at his house.

P. J's house was beautiful and big and so was his family. I grew to love his family because they were whole. He had his mom, dad, and several siblings. I loved that. Once inside, I saw a bunch of P.J.'s pictures. He gave me a tour of the house and had the privilege to see all the family pictures. Looking at his childhood pictures, one specifically with him, his sister, brothers, and his dad, made my heart warm. P.J. had a huge smile and looked every bit beautiful to me. Sometimes you could look at someone's picture and see the spirit of that person. Looking at that picture, I could sense that he was a loving little boy, and full of life. It was at that moment that I began to like him more and more.

In deep thought and concentration, I said to myself of how I wished to have known him at that moment in time because I would have loved him from a child. Oh my, how I loved him so. This was one of the happiest days I could remember with him and I. I remembered this day because we had so much fun. All day long we joked around, he introduced me to his friends, cousins, and vegetarian lifestyle. Not to mention, this was one of the first nights I spent with P.J. so that just made the entirety of the day even better. I know what you're thinking, how could my mother allow her 17-year-old daughter to spend the night with a boy? Calm your parenting 101 down.

For one, no I wasn't a nun, but sex was the furthest thing on my mind. For two, I was always open and honest with my mom, and very well-informed. Thus, spending the night was not an issue for my mom regarding me. My mother could trust me. As a side note, I later found out she allowed this because she thought he was gay. Boii, she couldn't be more wrong on that idea. I guess my mother took his mannerism and good looks to be a sign of homosexuality. When that was just his upbringing.

With this being the first night I slept over at P.J.'s house, I was a little nervous. I was very nervous to be exact, and although I loved and knew him, I wasn't one hundred percent sure about his family. I had watched too many movies on Lifetime Movie Network and was a little bit on guard. However, the day was wonderfully spent, as well as the night. The night was extremely hilarious because we had a play brawl. At a certain time during the night, P.J kept pushing for me to take a shower. I told him that I would. Consistent with his request, P.J. said for me not to be dirty and make it to the shower.

I chuckled and repeated that I would, but not at the moment. "Very well", replied P.J. Before I could catch my breath to make a slick retort, P.J. picked me up and carried me to the bathroom. I demanded that he put me down, fighting in every step, but he refused. P.J. then beckoned for his brother Mannie to help him out. "Excuse me", I screeched. Mannie came in, turned the shower on and P.J. threw me in the tub. Both brothers sealed the shower doors from the outside and threw a bar of soap over. I screamed for their mom, but no one came. The two were drenched in laughter and I was completely soaked.

I did not know how to operate their shower and was so focused on trying to get out, instead of turning all of my attention to turning the water off. His mother finally came in. Screaming loud and clear she yelled out his middle name. "Jayden!! What are you doing"? Seeing Ms. Janie's confusion made P.J., and his brother laugh even more. "Jamarra did not want to take a shower Mommie. We told her to take one before everyone else got in and we wanted the water to be warm for her" P.J. replied. Mrs. Janie began to laugh but just before walking away gave a stern demand.

"oh!!! Whatever mess is made you better clean it up" she insisted. After a few minutes, they released the doors and allowed me to step out. Being that I was drenched, I went to gather up my belongings to take a shower, but this meant war. Even with this, I could not help but laugh. When it was time to go to bed I slept on my side, and he slept on his side of the bed. I stated boundaries to make sure he didn't get any great ideas and his mother came in to wish us goodnight. We talked for about an hour or so and then went to sleep.

He never disrespected me once; he was the perfect gentleman. I was safe with him. At least I thought I was. A couple of weeks after this we took to sunset with a group of his friends. This would be the first time I ever rode a train, and it was with him. My mother took us to many places as a family and we traveled by road, but riding the rail was something simple, new, and yet so amazing for me. I was slowly falling in love but did not understand my feelings. Everything was going swell but then came an un-expectancy. He started dating. Everything happened so fast. Within a week, It went from, I met someone, to planning a day of intimacy.

I tried to cope with the way my emotions were spiraling as well as tell him how I felt, but it was too difficult to say. So, I went along with it. School mornings were the hardest because I would now have to see someone I loved; walking and holding hands with someone who was not me. Walking and holding someone else from behind. How did I get to this point?

CHAPTER FOUR

Playing with Fire

It was the week of prom. I was at the center of blessings and the world was at my feet. Young, beautiful, intelligent, and at the top of my class. Everything I prayed for had come to pass. My mother had taken me to this beautiful dress shop called Mod-Bella and brought me a dress of my liking. My sister had made sure that my hair was perfect, and my eyebrows queened. All that was left was my jewelry. I had an old friend take me to the prom and my P.J saw me off. I remember his face in amazement. He told me I was stunning.

I thought for a second, now he sees me. After prom, my date brought me back home. Dannie was the perfect gentleman and was head over heels for me. Dannie was the young man that most young women should choose. When I came home, to my surprise P.J was still there. My mother said he never left. To my surprise, he was keeping time. After the necessary preparations for bedtime P.J and I were together lying down in the Florida room, talking, and laughing like how we always did but this time it changed. P. J stated that if he wasn't in a relationship, he would kiss me.

I skipped the subject, and he said it again. I tried my best to avoid that topic because he did not know how tempting this was for me. Especially, since I was crazy for him. I tried to veer off the topic but P.J said again this time slowly and passionately ringing in my heart. "Jalaina, if I were not in a relationship, I would kiss you".

I leaned forward, grabbed his shirt, and kissed him. Looking into his eyes I knew what this feeling was. I was completely and incandescently in love with P.J. In the middle of the night, P.J woke me up with a kiss. As I was receptive and kissed back, he climbed on top of me and began kissing me passionately. I had my first kiss before, yes, but nothing like this. Not this feeling. The next morning, I felt like crap, and he did also, we sat out by the poolside and were both in a deep quiet. He had to tell Bella that he cheated on her and that I assisted him. I assisted in hurting someone. This thought alone taunted my mind.

The next school day had arrived, and it was confession time. My emotions were wrapped up in my stomach. I had gone to speak to Bella face to face after having sent her a long text for P.J. I took most of the blame for everything, letting her know it didn't mean anything. Oh, great so now I'm a liar. I told her what a young lady would want to hear after being cheated on. I said things that will give her some type of assurance. At the end of the day Bella accepted P. J's apology and my confession. It felt as if with all the mess in the air, the other two sides of this triangle were satisfied, while I was the one left to hurt.

When I asked him at the pool side what would be our next move and he replied that he would tell Bella the truth and how he was so very afraid of what her response would be; I knew that I would have to take over the situation. At the end of the day all I could ask myself was how was this happening? This was my last year of high school, and I have managed to fall in love with someone who does not even know that I love them. On top of this he is very much unavailable for that matter.

I wanted to bawl up and cry. In that instant of sadness, I began to remember when P.J pulled me close and kissed me. Meditating on this was as if I was at that black gate again watching the sunset. As a little girl there was a tall gate down the street from me. It divided the avenue. I would race to it at a certain time to climb up and beat the sun before it sets. Up so high and holding on watching the sunset was the most beautiful thing in the world to me at that age. This is how I felt that day. I felt that at that moment, I was denying the truth.

That the kiss I was denying was the most beautiful thing to me and although it was wrong, at that moment, for that moment it was mines. With all this confusion, the thing I feared most was, would I ever get to taste his lips again, would that moment ever happen again. For a while I tried to avoid P.J. I stopped answering his calls and texts. My mom inquired about what was happening, but I just simply told her that I was upset with him. This was the truth. I was upset. I was upset and crushed. After some time, we started speaking again as friends. Although P.J was still holding onto how I abruptly stopped all communication, with proper communication, set boundaries and apologies, we began the relationship back as if nothing ever had happened.

Things were going straight and narrow for a while as far as our best friendship was concerned until one day I slipped. I slipped up and spoke up. P.J and I was outside at my mother's house when we had got into an argument about something minor. While in the mist of the disagreement he turned around to walk away, and I yelled out that I was in love with him. I blurted out without remorse of tone; "It's not you, it's me. It's because I'm in love with you." P.J stopped walking and said nothing at first.

The way his countenance looked depleted, made my heart sank into my stomach. What would he say back? How did those words leave my mouth? After these questions choked me for two minutes straight, I swallowed hard and told him to forget it. I will not go another day without the truth known. I held my head up high and waited for his response. Directing his attention to the ground then back up at me, P.J asked why? "Didn't I tell you not to fall in love with me", he softly mentioned with respect of tone. This soft reply spiraled me down a loud memory lane. Causing me to remember the first night I spent with him.

Remembering of how him and I were joking around and talking just before going to sleep, when he told me not to fall in love with him. I remember laughing and informing him to make sure he utilized that same advice. At that moment in time, I loved him as a person, but I was not in love. Snapping back to reality from memory lane I looked up at him strong but felt slightly defeated. Remembering this, made a harsh sting in my heart like a bee- sting on the right butt cheek, or more like a slap in the face. After a few moments of piercing silence, P.J turned around to walk into the house.

Instead of leaving in anger he stayed, but just like that passionate kiss that night, we acted as if nothing was said or done. Days after this I felt free like something was off my chest but still groggy. P.J called me, I thought it was to discuss my confession, but it was to speak about his present relationship. Just great, not only was I pining over this dude, but I also had to play like someone's love specialist as well. P.J informed me of how Bella's and his relationship was on and off, that nothing he was doing seemed to please her.

Like someone in love I took the hurt. Like a best friend I gave him advice on how to keep her. Yes, I was in love, but I loved him enough to help him even if it meant putting my wants to the side. This same cycle went on for a while, and I wondered if I would ever receive the same respect in return. Life has its ups and downs, but at this time it felt as down was the new normal for me. One day on my way home from school, I received devastating news that my cousin Jeremy had been killed. My cousin had lived with us for a while and then moved out, so this hit close to home for me.

Jeremy was a little older than myself, but I never saw it as that. Some of the family may have viewed him as trouble, but I saw a sweet kid, who loved his mom but just had some rough patches that he could not understand. Back when mom would take me to Auntie Paula's house and everything was beautiful amongst our family, Jeremy and I would share awesome childhood moments with one another. As a child Jeremy was so sweet, and innocent. We loved riding bikes together and looking at his beautiful car collection. After a while, things went sour, and .my mom and aunt became distant.

This caused a pause between Jeremy's and I relationship, but the love never died. After a few years later, life brought us back together, but things were very different. Jeremy moved in my mom's house but then he quickly moved out. Even with this, I still saw Jeremy as that sweet little boy with the car collection who was taken away from this world prematurely. To get the call that he was killed came ripping through me like a bad stomachache. I cried so hard that my chest started hurting. When P.J heard the news, he came over to provide comfort, during which, he spent the entire day as well as night with me.

I remembered this night to be one of the roughest nights during my grieving period, because I had a bad dream about my cousin Jeremy. In my dream, I was calling out to him, but he didn't respond. In the dream it's like his spirit was taunting me and mocking the hurt I felt about his lost. Then suddenly, I felt something wrap its arms around me. I went from feeling alone and afraid during the dream to feeling safe and warm. When I woke up, P.J had me in his arms cuddling me. I moved and asked what happened, and by my facial expression, P.J quickly explained himself. Stating how I was tossing and turning, and he only thought to hold me.

"I lost a family member who I loved dearly, and I wished someone would have been there for me" he said, with a sincere, yet sad visage. Vowing to be there with me through every step of the way, P.J. words rendered tremendous console to me. In that moment I knew without a shadow of a doubt, that I had a true friend. This is what layered the icing on the cake. This is what made me love him more. I loved the fact that when I needed him, he was front and center. Weeks passed and P.J was helping me cope. Whenever I felt like reverting back in my mind he was there. This made me appreciate him so much more. We went swimming, dinning out, painting, I even met him at his job and was able to help him close out sometimes.

The pain seemed to ease up a bit and my Graduation was very near. With just the thought of graduation made me super excited but afraid as well. This was a huge milestone and pathway into adulthood. I would miss the safety and security high school offered. Not to mention, things were getting a little rocky with my mom as far as work was concerned and my sister had a beautiful baby boy for me to completely love. He was like sitting on a porch swing eating ice cream on a warm sunny day.

I loved my little naked bandit. P.J loved him as well. I loved how he helped me look after my nephew. This often caused me to be stuck in spells thinking of a family with him. P. J's charm and care with my nephew, reminded me of that night, and passionate kiss. Our relationship as best friends bloomed prettier than a field of roses in its season. Graduation was a few days away; I was cruising with my mom to family members house to spend quality time when Janeisha text me that my cousin Carl was killed. I couldn't believe it and at the same time I found it difficult to breathe.

I ran to my mom and informed her of the text message I received and stated that we had to go. On the way to the house my mom kept saying that it was not true, he was not gone, and that you don't get that kind of thing in a text. As she was talking all I saw was him and I at grandma's house sleeping on that beautiful rug she had with the seven kids praying. I re-envisioned the times of me chasing him around the house and sitting up on the back wall of my house talking for hours. This could not be, just a week prior to this he was demanding graduation tickets from me. Both of our graduations were scheduled in June. Carl's Graduation was June 7th and mines was the 9th. Someone killed my cousin the 2nd of June.

Carl was on the way home from school. At first there were many accusations. Some family members thought he was in a gang. I quickly knew that was not the case. Not Carl. All those voices and silly speculations came to a hush when we heard the truth. If I never knew hate before, I learned it on June 2ND. I hated the man that took his life, that so much if I could have had my way, I would have erased every trace of him from the earth. Some people talk about killing a person in return but not me.

I envisioned being able to make it that he was never born along with his entire generation. Yeap!! I told you I was a different kind of weird. During the investigation my mom said they believed it was a mistaken identity. My whole heart felt as it was ripped out. All on the account of mistaken identity our family lost a son, grandson, nephew, and beloved cousin. Everyone loved Carl. Carl would go to my grandmother's house just to wash her dishes and help out around the house. Carl was a great worker, gentleman, son, grandson, and cousin, when he didn't have to be but wanted to.

Carl was great at everything, and they took him from us. I never wanted to hurt anyone. I never dreamed of wanting true revenge until then. Every day and hour after that day, I felt it on my chest. Time seemed to be like it was slowed down, and things started happening with my mom. The night of Carl's death she tried to harm herself. The night of his death it felt like everyone around me was worried about themselves, and I was just trying to breathe. After the hospital when I reached home, I showered, and then found a text from P. J. The next day he rushed over. He was with me through this as well.

I went to graduation and wept through graduation and mom was still very different. There were so many things going on, along with my mom not working anymore. She got into a case on her job with a woman. A woman lied on her, and it took them two and a half years to investigate the truth. Meanwhile, I was slowly losing my mom to depression, anxiety, financial situations, and worry. Thank you, U.S. Postal Service. If I had the time to write a book separately on the emotional turmoil that job had caused my mother, the government would perhaps find another way to deliver mail.

Nah!! Who am I kidding as if they would truly care. A few weeks passed but P.J. stayed close. I started going out with my family and one-night P.J. told me that I was changing. P.J explained that this frightened him because it was almost like I didn't care anymore. For a short period, I didn't. Carl was gone, the everyday visits to the graveyard, never spoke back, my mom was acting differently, very different, and on top of that I was in love with someone that was not in love with me in return.

Yeah!! Different/changing/and not giving a crap pretty much summed it up. After thinking of these things, I glanced back at him and chuckled. Reading the pain behind my laugh; he grabbed me, held me close, and told me he didn't want to lose me. After this he followed those words up with a kiss. P.J pulled me away from his chest, grabbed my face to look in my eyes and kissed me several times. For a few days after that and every day after that, we kissed. We kissed until we were out of breath. We kissed until we both came to turns that we would stop. After all, he was still in a relationship.

When things couldn't get any more confusing an old friend showed up. This old friend from elementary came around and turned my selfishness upside down, sit back and let me tell ya bout it. As stated, we had known each other for years and he had his very own name for me. The name was simple, the name was sweet, the name also contained my favorite color. "Blue Jay!!! Come go to the beach with me and my friends," said Landon. "For sure just let me grab my things" I replied. At the beach we threw a fire, laughed, and talked crap. I was going through a lot but did not want to talk about grief and hate. I wanted normal again. This old friend leaned in and kissed me.

Confused at first but didn't care about the next. I thought what the heck and kissed him back. The day was short lived, I came home early. The next day I woke up to a text from Henry. The text plainly read "How are you doing baby"? From a kiss to him calling me his girlfriend the very next day. Yes, Jaliana that pretty much how it works, I thought to myself. So, I went with it. I didn't understand the me at the time, but like music I thought to just go with the flow. Hey, I have a boyfriend now. P.J came over and I introduced him to my new good- looking.

P.J had looked like someone had slapped him with a pogo stick. A nice week had passed, and I spent time with solely my guy. I needed to speak to P.J to set boundaries, but before the conversation could ever arise, I came home from a day out to find P.J on the couch waiting and watching T.V. Could this be the time to tell him? P.J beckoned me over to watch a show and I obliged. Nighttime came and I went to my room and closed the door. Maybe this would paint the picture I thought. Usually when P.J would spend the night, I would sleep on my floor pad right next to the couch that he would lay on in the Florida room.

That way we would be near one another. I will explain the pad on the floor. It's not that he wasn't a gentleman, it's that I was not allowing anyone to really sleep on my floor pad. I slept with my mom until about sixteen, close to seventeen years old. When she kicked me out of her room, I did not smoothly transition back to mine, so I slept on a floor pad in the florida room, to be closer to her. This served as a pacifier but gave me a new attachment (The pad). The pad was very comfortable and that became my sleeping place. The rest is history. In the middle of that very night P.J came inside my room and laid down in my bed.

I turned and asked, "what are you doing"? P.J leaned in to kiss me. I moved out the way and said, "No" also reminding him that I was in a relationship. P.J then retorted that when he was in a relationship, I could kiss him. I felt like a bruised hypocrite. "Fine just kiss me then". As P. J's lips touched mine, I did not kiss back but pushed him off instead and said, "No this is not me". I called up Landon that same minute to let him know that I could not be with him. Informing him that I was in love with P.J and that I did not wish to hurt him in any fashion. The next morning Landon came to visit me. We spoke face to face.

Landon confessed that he was in love with me. I replied since when, because we were only together for a short time frame. Landon told me since elementary. He said he loved me since forever. I felt like a complete bad guy. I apologized again and before leaving, Landon said goodbye and kissed my forehead. I thought back to before all of this when I had morals. I did not play with people's emotions, and if ever I felt the need to cheat on someone, I would break up with them first. I created and followed my own code. Although I did break up with Landon, this feeling crippled me and showed me just how truly selfish I was at the time.

I loved Landon but not in the way he loved me. I regretted that I ever allowed the relationship. I knew I was in love with P.J before I ever let Landon kiss me and for that I was just as worse as the manipulation played by P.J that night. Hey if I'm going to tell it, I might as well tell it all, right? I understood completely now what I was doing to P. J's girl. No more. This was selfishness. From that day on I was committed to doing the right thing. I told P.J that as long as he was in a relationship this whole cheating business was out of the question.

I don't care that her and him was off and on again and that's the times when we would kiss. As far as I was concerned my lips was Switzerland. Too far and out of the question. I had hurt someone I truly loved as a friend. Yes, I was in a grieving state at the moment but that was still no excuse. I felt like a douche bag, and I never wanted to feel that way again. Yes, hurt people hurt people but it doesn't make it expedient or right. It just makes an excuse and an unprofitable one on both ends.

I was done with playing with fire. I told him I was moving on. I meant that. I made up in my mind that because of what I had did to P. J's girl and Landon, that I would stay single. I was going to stay single until I could change the type of love I had for P.J, erase that part and then move on. Close one door before I opened any other doors. Little did I know that's not how it truly works. Let me explain. When you truly love someone, and you are in love with them, time does not erase. Only actions do; but even with that, being in love can change but loving someone does not.

Once you really love someone, you can fall out of love but loving the person that feeling stays. Not love because of sex, or love because of money, but loving someone simply because of their soul and who they are; that is unerasable. There is no erasing that. P.J and I spent time together. The more time we spent the more he trusted me. I begin learning inner secrets. Like for instance P.J quit his job and started selling Marijuana. I never knew he smoked at all. He then introduced me to the smoker's case. Where your lips never turn black, eyes are never dilated, and you smell sweeter than clothes that freshly leave the dryer. I thought he was small time, but I was so very wrong about this thought.

I figured in my mind it was just a phase, because we both went to a very strict and well-known high school and when we attended, I never witnessed that on him. I was mind boggled, but I was his best friend. The most I did was give him advice. P.J laughed and said, "Jalaina don't tell me you thought that all the money I had come from that job". P.J worked at a very high-end job that paid him well. I never suspected anything else. Besides that, I never counted his pockets. That was the furthest thing from my mind. My mother never had me around that lifestyle.

I had homeboys that dibbled in smoking Mary Jane and my brother trifled a little with it, but they always respected me and never brought that stuff around me. One day P.J brought over a weed brownie. He explained that he was trying something new and wanted to see how it was. For he never dabbled with edibles. I said let me try a piece just to see. I wanted to see what the hype was about. I took a piece, but it did absolutely nothing, I laughed at him. I thought in my head this young boy doesn't know what he is doing. This was just a phase. This all will change. I thought.

CHAPTER FIVE

Crutch to Confession

Close to a year had passed since the Landon situation, and it was a little before my 19th birthday that I began speaking to a gentleman as a friend only. Sure, he had expressed that he was very fond of me, but I told him I was not looking for a relationship and I meant that. Even with my statements the gentleman became very serious about me. We were just getting to know one another solely through friendship, but this young man spoke of relationship and marriage every chance he could. P.J caught wind of this through a phone conversation I was having and as the days progressed, he grew more curious about my friendship with the gentleman.

P.J. and I continuously spent an ample amount of time with one another. We were inseparable, but I went about our friendship the correct way this time around. Then one weekend day, P.J. and I were headed to his best friend's house to chill. Everything was cool that day until he began nitpicking at me about the littlest things. I inquired of him for the reason as to why he was trying to pick a fight and consistently mentioning my new friend. After questioning him, he turned towards me and simply expressed that it wasn't my new friend and that it wasn't even me, but it was more so of the fact that he was in love with me. P.J. explained that he had been in love with me for a long time, but he knew that expressing this to me would not have changed anything.

I could not believe the words that came out of his mouth. This whole time he was in love and said nothing. I was relieved and confused, while at the same time also curious as to why? Why now? I asked about Bella he said that Bella and he were separated. I didn't understand why would him being in love with me not change anything? I wish I had asked that question then? Instead, I asked if he was sure of his feelings because I completely stepped back from him in that manner and did not wish to hurt anyone nor did I want any more parts of that.

He expressed that they were over. We left his friend's house, and he came back to my house. Spoke some more about the situation and sealed our conversation off with an agreement to be together. I called up the young man that I was getting acquainted with to inform him that I was now in a relationship and that things would have to shift out of respect for my guy. I explained to him that although we were friends, I understood that he wanted more, and that friendship would not or could not continue. Friendship is okay, you don't just cut people off, but his intentions were not just solely for friendship, and I wasn't going to disrespect my relationship with P.J.

Yes, some may say that this was wrong, and yes, some may say that I was selfish; but the heart wants what it wants. The gentleman expressed to me that although he and I were not in a relationship, he was truly hurt. I truly apologized and wished him well. The very next day, I phoned all the people nearest to me and let them know of this beautiful confession. I felt as if I made it to the clouds without a plane. I felt like I was on my way into a forever love. A love, a marriage, children, and a forever of being in the arms of a young man that already had a huge part of me (my heart).

I was on top of the world. A few weeks passed and we enjoyed one another. We went on dates, etc. Then one night, P.J. called me and asked if we could go out to speak privately. We ended up going to Morningside, a beautiful place where the ocean meets the park. We sat at a picnic table that was perfectly shaded by a tree close to the ocean. I always loved sitting there with P.J. because we seldom climbed the tree together. I felt so joyful and as if nothing around me existed, not even gravity.

Was this possible? While we were sitting there, I noticed that P.J. seemed a little off. Before asking him anything, I decided to stay quiet and let him speak if he wanted to. P.J. then grabbed my hands and asked me if I knew about polygamy. I told him yes. He then sighed heavily and asked about my views on it. I told him that I didn't believe in it, but I understood that it was practiced in some countries. P.J. then quickly explained that he was in love with me but also in love with Bella. At that moment, the cloud, the world, gravity, and everything surrounding them appeared suddenly. So fast that it was on top of me.

As P.J called my name, I swallowed the pain to regain the strength to speak. What? What is he talking about, where was this all coming from? Why is my heart racing? And then finally, I said "okay. I'll do this for you". When those words left my mouth, it was like my heart bit my tongue. Why did I lie? For my answer was yes but in my heart the answer was no. I found myself asking where was the strong Jamarra? When I used to date before him, the minute I saw a red flag, I would break off the relationship and have another suitor in the next two weeks. I was carefree, adventurous, and untouched. This night I felt like a kitten in a yard of dogs.

This night the unbreakable me, felt breakable. In that instant, P.J called up Bella to ask her the same question, and like many rational human beings, she was furious, declined the offer and cursed him out. P.J explained how his parents practiced polygamy. Well, his dad had started the entire thing at first and his mom came around to it, or should I say had no other choice but to make a stay or leave decision. This is when that unasked question rang in mind. The question that I never asked. If he was in love with me as well, why wouldn't that have changed things?

The truth was he was somehow in love with two people at once and he knew that this wouldn't be accepted. Therefore, he never confessed to me his true feelings because his feelings came with an exception. P.J was confused, and my heart left as a subject to confusion. Everything that had transpired after this was a blur. So much of a blur that I can't even write about it. I could not get out of my head why I said that I would consider polygamy. Although she said no, and I could have him to myself; did I really have him? The one that I once felt safe with just took a wrong turn down a one-way street.

After a few days, P.J told me he was completely over Bella, that she didn't love him enough to say yes, but I did. Some time had passed a few months and things felt normal again. His birthday was arriving, and I wanted to make him smile. He once told me that because he had such a big family that a lot of times, they shared their birthday months. From this I thought to highlight him. So, I did what any young person in love would do. I threw him a party. I purchased everything and asked a loved one to cook for me. I had vegetarian lasagna salad and dinner rolls on the menu.

Along with this, I had a fruit platter arranged and brought a cake. After the food was taken care of, I phoned most of his loved ones and close friends. The party was magnificent. P. J was taken back. No one had ever done that for him. I thought from that moment, all the love I had I could just pour it into him. In hopes of filling every part of him that was empty, I would love. Besides that's what love does, right. It heals? I thought that he would change. I knew I couldn't change him, but I did believe that love could. Motivational speakers always say you can't change a man. However, people change every day if they have something to change for.

I also faulted his parents for the confusion of polygamy. Time passed, P.J and I shared beautiful times. Fishing, climbing, gardening, watching movies and so on. After a year of dating, dry-humping, and kisses, the conversation of sex was in the air. P.J was not a virgin, but I was. I always wanted to wait for marriage. I thought something as sacred as that could wait. So, it was going to have to wait. I went to Janeisha's house to spend time with her. Janeisha was my perfect little doll baby. Although we were adults that's how I viewed her. I loved Janeisha and If I could help it, I wouldn't let any harm come to her.

I confided in Janeisha about waiting for sex, my fear of losing P.J., and how I did little things to suffice him. Janeisha quickly said how it was not fair to him and how eventually those little things would not be enough. Hurt and scared, I replied with a "Not true", quickly stating to Janeisha how I believed it was enough. Janeisha then pitched the perfect ice cream analogy. She explained while questioning me at the same time, if I would like for someone to offer me an ice cream cone, but only allow for me to have a few licks.

'No of course not", I said. Exactly, she retorted. This is what you're doing to him. Janeisha stated that if I had loved him, I would need to make the decision, that it was my choice, but I couldn't expect him to sit around and wait. I was at a feeling of wishing I had someone to talk to. I usually would run to my mom, but I knew or thought her opinion would be biased. When P.J. and I made our relationship official, I immediately told my mom. However, her attitude towards him started to change, which upset me because of the negative things she would say about him.

Despite the fact that P.J. was a financial help to my mother and always there for me, my mother became indifferent towards him once the relationship began. As a result, I felt like I had no one to talk to about my relationship. Even though I could have confided in my mother's best friend, I was afraid of being judged, since I had always been known to give advice on premarital sex. I found myself struggling with conflicting thoughts and was unable to sleep that night after leaving Janeisha's house. I knew that I would eventually have to ask P.J a question that I didn't want to hear the answer for.

I knew I was in love, but at that moment, a lot of questions came up. The biggest one was why love was so hard when I gave it so freely. It was my first lesson in understanding that giving love freely didn't mean it had to be reciprocated on the same level. In simple terms, not everyone has the same mindset or expresses love in the same way as you. The thought of sex made me afraid, and I knew it was time to have a conversation with my mom. Yes, you read that right. I had always told my mom I would wait until marriage but being that I felt so deeply for P.J; things came into play such as sacrifices.

After having the conversation with my mom about a week after I asked P.J if he would be able to wait until marriage. He let me know, that he couldn't. All the wisdom and knowledge that I had flew out the door. Before P.J. came into my life, I would end a relationship with any guy who mentioned sex to turn around and have someone else within two weeks. I used to advise young women and older women alike to ditch any man who couldn't wait. Hmm all that quickly changed. When you're in love, so far in and too close, things change. But was this the right type of love? A decision had to be made. My rationalization behind the decision was an echoing question; is it worth it?

CHAPTER SIX

Are You Ready?

A few weeks had passed, and it was time to address the issue that grabbed my stomach. I made up my mind but needed clarity on his part. I grabbed P.J by his hands and took him to the upstairs room in his parents' house. I like this room/office. It was decorated so beautifully, and the sun hit it just right. I climbed on top of him, looked him in the eyes, and asked him with all sincerity, "Are you ready"? I told him that once I give my virginity to him and we marry that it would be until death do us part.

I questioned to make sure if he was sure of the commitment, was there anything I needed to know, did he perhaps still have feelings for Bella, or is this a go. P.J was always honest, so I took his word. He closed his eyes, nodded his head, opened his eyes, and said yes. From that day I made up in my mind that it was time that I would give myself to him. I just didn't know when. A few weeks after my 20th birthday, I was spending time with P.J in the upper room.

I remember this day as a Saturday at the beach with my toes in the sand. I had on a long blue and white skirt on, with a white tank top. My hair was braided in Platts. P.J had his hair up and he smelled very neutral. I love to take in the scent of people, so that I could always remember them. P.J and I were kissing then other things. One thing led to the next and I gave him the que. I remembered taking a deep breath, the pressure, the hurt, the feeling, and then saying to him after releasing my breath, "you're in"?

It was not that I didn't feel him, it was more of the fact that I couldn't believe that something I was holding like a glass case for years, was given to someone in seconds. Besides I was only 20 years young (to me I was still a child inside). On that day, we made love. It was the day I made a sacrifice, the day I took a step towards a different kind of relationship. That night, I didn't even go into my room. Instead, I laid down on the red-based multicolored couch in the living room by the front door, where I curled up in a fetal position, and cried on the inside. I was scared. The next morning, I woke up sore and went to wash up and get ready.

I was going out of town to visit Janeisha, who had gone off to college. I had wanted to go with her, but my mom asked me to stay, so I did. Besides that, there were a few other reasons I stayed back. I stayed back for Mom, P.J., my best friend, and the fear of failing. After Janeisha had spent some time at the university, I decided to go and see her. If I'm not mistaken, she had already spent a year and some time in school, so this visit was long overdue. As I rode on the Greyhound, flashbacks of when I initially drove up the road with Janeisha and her mom to view one of the universities that had accepted us came to mind.

Conversations and events from that trip came running through my mind, as well as the thought of how different life would have been if I had accepted the acceptance letter. I remember telling Janeisha of how I would attend the university with her. That we would be together. With my scores on the A.C.T assessment and graduating as magma cum laude; yeah. yah girl had choices to go anywhere, even Vanderbilt. I remember Janeisha- saying "no you are not, and that at the end of the day you will stay down with your mom if asked to do so".

Janeisha was right, but This was before P.J and I were even in a relationship; this was before losing my virginity; this was before a lot of things. As I snapped back to reality the fear crept in again, so, I decided to call P.J. I called several times, but he didn't answer, which I found to be strange because he always answered. Janiesha picked me up from the greyhound with her boyfriend. On the way to their place, Janeisha could sense that something was wrong and after questioning me, I told her everything. She looked very shocked at first but in the next minute blurted out in laughter saying that my cobwebs were finally gone.

With a defeated countenance, I told her that he wasn't answering the phone. Rob tuned into the conversation out of concern, where they both agreed that he was busy and not to worry. After my third day with Janiesha and Rob, it was time to leave. On the way back, I finally received a phone call from P.J. I asked why he didn't answer the phone, and in response he told me that he was very busy but also very upset with me. P.J explained that you don't do something like what we did and take off the next day. I didn't know how to respond because everything was new to me. There's no class that can teach you how to feel or act after losing your virginity.

Yes, there are sex education classes that provide safety measures and precautions, but not guidance on emotions or behavior. Besides, I was an adult. Over the next two weeks, we spent a lot of time together and explored each other. It became easier each time, but the conviction grew heavier, especially at the thought of having to inform my mom. I talked to P.J. about my feelings and suggested we practice celibacy, but he never responded. Communicating was usually easy, but it's difficult to explain something like this to someone who can't understand or respect you on a spiritual level.

With dealing with the uneasiness of the mind concerning this new change with me, it was time to speak to my mom. I was trying to think of a smooth and calm way, but that conversation never came; well smoothly that is. Picture this, a nice day at work, stocking shelves at the local Winn-Dixie. My job was to clean, stock, rotate and rid expired goods. While working and pulling out pallets from the back, I hear my name called over the loudspeaker. "Jamarra, come to the front please, Jamarra come to the front".

As I approached the front counter Ms. Patricia explained that my mom was on the phone. I was wondering why she would call the store versus my cellular. Mom had called to ask some store sales questions. After these questions I tried to scurry off the phone, when I was quickly interrupted by another question. My mom had asked "Jalaina what time are you coming home tonight?" I replied that I wasn't coming home, and that I would be with P.J. Over the lovely black Winn-Dixie phone, my mother Janie decided to ask the most outrageous question.

"Jalaina baby I hope you not having sex with this boy"? Instead of saying mom I will call you back, A quick yes, we did so recently, we used protection and that I would speak to you soon, came out of my mouth. My mom went crazy. I basically inherited every bad name in the book. As she was acting an entire fool over the phone; I wanted to say do you see how enraged you are? just as enraged as you are, is just as afraid as I am. I wanted to tell her how instead of her yelling I wish she would have held me or conversated with me instead. That was one of the biggest decisions of my life at the time and I needed her. I didn't say that though. I just said I will call you back mom. A couple of weeks after this mom was still acting sour.

She was acting very mean. Don't get me wrong before losing my virginity she was already behaving like a sour puss. How is it I'm going to a prestigious University, making A'S and B's, helping with my nephew, working, and walking to school and she found room to nag me? Deflection was the word. Mom was at a place of no income, dealing in a relationship where the male was the bread winner (in which she was not use to), on top of this he would always evoke all of the ways he assists her whenever he was inebriated.

At the time I didn't realize mom was attacking me because she was worried not just for herself but for me as well. I didn't understand that. I mean, I understood there were financial issues but if we were on the streets, it would be me and mom on the streets together. I never understood mom until I was able to. So, at the time I just felt attacked. Then when I lost my virginity, she made me feel unwanted and attacked. The arguments kept getting worse, so I moved out and in with a loved one. I thought this would help salvage our relationship, but I was wrong. Mom followed me there to argue with me, and I knew that I would have to leave there, but I didn't want to go back home.

At the time I felt that I couldn't. To put the cheery on top of the cake something else happened. It was on a sunny afternoon, after having tidied up my family's house, I had driven over to P. J's house just to relax and lay down with him. As I was laying on his chest, gently tracing his black Chinese tattoos, he began to speak to me. Words, commas, fragments, and periods never came alive in a sentence for me until then. "Jalaina, I have something to tell you. I am in love with Arabella Elena Perez. She was my morning cup of coffee". When this was said my fingers went from tracing to limp.

As P.J continued to speak to me, I just listened and everything all my senses were heightened. "Every morning before school I would stop at McDonald's so I could get her pancakes and a cup of coffee." Just to see her smile." P.J softly spoke, while tearing pieces of my heart away bit by bit. Has someone ever cut you so deep in your feeling that your mouth watered, a sharp pain lashed across your throat; and the only thing one could do is allow the tears to run down unannounced?

As I tried to muster up the strength to speak, all that came out was, "you said that you were ready". P.J then replied, "I know; it's just I do love you and I didn't want to see you with or even marry that guy." "I didn't want to lose you and I know it was selfish, but I couldn't and wouldn't lose you." I laid there and couldn't move. It was as if I was completely paralyzed. All I could do is cry and lay sore. My entire body was hurting. How could this be? I did not cry out for mom, most definitely not my dad, neither could I cry out for me. I did not feel me. At that moment, my confidence, my pride, my strength, my joy, my bubbliness, my breath, everything in me had left.

So, I laid there and cried as he laid on the side of me. As the tears slowly slipped down my face P.J Continued to speak. Pain set in like a studious student taking a four-hour assessment. I never wanted to be a lawyer, nor did I ever imagine taking the assessment that gives them their credentials; but I could now imagine sitting in for the Uniform Bar Examination. I imagined it to be throat busting. Like being choked while still having the capability of breathing (torture). Every bit of pain was felt all at once. I told P.J that if he wanted, I could try to get him them back together.

I told him that I would write to her and then I would just leave. "No!!!, he expounded. "Bella would never take me back anyhow". After a while of lying there, I mustered up the strength so that I could get up from the bed, walk down those wood stairs and drive back to my family's house. At the time I had a small little Camry. As I reached back home, I yearned for warmth. So, I headed for the shower. Nothing like a hot shower to wash away the emptiness and good sleep to temporarily numb the pain. Before laying down, P.J had rung several times. After a while had passed, I finally answered the phone.

P.J was frantic saying for us to stay together. P.J desperately mentioned that he did not know why he said those things and he could not lose me. He said he did not know why he was like this. I found myself going back. I didn't understand it, but I didn't want him to hurt. I figured this is what I had deserved for everything that I did before this, and although I was hurting, I didn't want him to hurt. I even somehow blamed his family and myself for what transpired. I believed I deserved it. I blamed his family because there was a lot of confusion in how he was raised but this was their way of life (marijuana and polygamy).

Ms. Janie did not accept polygamy, but it was done behind her back for years. The children found out and then eventually she did as well. The situation unraveled with her going through motions and then the acceptance of it. With an understanding of confusion that P.J was subject too, I thought maybe If I poured in enough love, I could change the way he saw some things. I would give it my all, besides, I had already given a good 80% of me already. I decided that I would love him through whatever this was.

With all of this, P.J was consistently asking for me to move in, and considering what was happening at my loved one's house this idea wasn't a far fetch. I did not want to move in with P.J but I didn't want to trouble Skarlet any longer. I wasn't so much that I was a burden, it was the fact that her relatives made complaints about it. I didn't have to leave necessarily, but I knew it wasn't fair for me to make her choose between me and her blood family. So, I eventually caved in and moved in with P.J. I remembered while driving to PJ's house, before coming up to that left corner to turn down his street, the Lord spoke to me and said that I was not ready.

I replied back, 'Yes I am. I can cook, I can clean, I won't cheat, Yeah, I am ready! I heard the Lord say you have no idea. For that day, that was the last time I heard from Abba. Upon moving in. P.J was helping me to unload. Our little place was to the back. His parents had a very huge house. Their house was like an entire building so that everyone could have their own private area away from that of the mom and dad. To me this was clever. To me it was different. The parents had designated us a small space to the back of the house, where we would share with one other relative. It was three rooms, one bathroom and a stove.

CHAPTER SEVEN

Monster Moves

Looking at the space to configure how I would mesh mines with his, I thought of the perfect idea. As I sat on the floor loading some of my things in the drawer, P.J walked into the room upset, grabbed the draw that I was loading and emptied all the stuff out onto the floor. Very startled, I asked him what were the reasons behind his actions? That day was pretty much a blur, but after a serious conversation with him, he apologized and stated how he was just not used to living with someone.

I was puzzled, and really thrown aback because this was the same person begging me to move in with him. Nevertheless, we kissed and made up. For a few weeks things were beautiful. We went to picnics at the park, the movies, and the whole nine. We shared picnic days, outside adventures, Netflix, and chill nights, and the regular out to eat. Going out to eat was the most difficult at times because he was vegetarian, and I was only pescatarian. All my life I consumed whatever I wanted, but once entering the relationship with P.J I turned pescatarian. I was willing to become pescatarian for two reasons.

One reason was that P.J stated how no wife of his would eat meat. From a conversation, and with the facts laid out on the table, I agreed to converting. P.J explained he never consumed meat a day in his life and how it would be almost lethal without a doctor's trial. It was more suitable for me to convert, on top of this, the entire family were vegetarians, and that's how he would want his kids brought up. Secondly, I had gained a bit of weight after high school with the help of improper eating and steroid consumption for a couple of months due to illness. So, I used this reasoning to sacrifice and forfeit meats. Understanding that in a serious relationship, there would be compromises that had to be made. However, I did not notice that I was the only one compromising. The first few weeks after our first mishap were like honeymoon beautiful but excitement was short lived.

Things started changing. It's like after I lost my virginity to him and things started unfolding, secrets began to come out. Things I never knew and had no idea about started to surface. P.J would look at me and tell me sometimes that he was like an onion and that there were too many layers. However, I believed that he would change. I wanted him to change like a cold drink after a good workout, but my thirst was never quenched. After a couple of months things took a turn for the worse. I ended up leaving my job at Winn-Dixie. We received new management and the new manager kept playing with my hours and deliberately making it for my school time.

While I was at work, the head honcho was always on my aisle instead of working. I was very responsible with great work ethics, but this man always found a reason to be on my isle. Something was completely wrong with this guy. He would set my hours for school hours and call me in class. I had enough of that. So, I put in a two week resignation and began to look for another job. I know before leaving a job you should already have another secured, but I was completely fed up. After leaving Winn-Dixie I looked for jobs but when there was no good turnaround for work, things really began unfolding.

45

P.J started making fast big money and his attitude began to change. Then when things did not get any better, worse followed and heart tare came knocking back at my door again. One day we were going to go out. P.J had walked out the room to get a few things before we left. His phone kept going off from text messages, which I wouldn't usually pay no mind too. For he was a dealer. Plus, I would never go through no one's phone. I felt like if you have to go through someone's phone, just leave. Violating personal space makes you just as worse.

However, this day was different, his phone was face up and I was picking it up to leave out the door. The message showed up on the screen". I can't wait to see you ". It was from a young lady named Paula. I grew leery because something just didn't feel right. P.J had large clientele, so he received many weird messages. Even when we would drop off in person the way people would act about his product, was insane, but it was something about this text I couldn't shrug off. The uneasy feeling did not bulge, but I was not going to go inside his phone and read through his messages.

So, I decided that when we come back from grabbing lunch that I would have a conversation with him. As we drove around to go for our Publix sub, we began to speak about everything like we always did. We spoke on life, future, the silly things that made us laugh and the things that were the most definite violation to us. I told P.J I always appreciate honesty in everything. From saying that, he immediately turned around and said Jalaina I cheated on you. I closed my eyes, took a deep breath, and said "excuse me". P.J said Paula came to the house around the back looking for a dime from Tony (Tony was P. J's oldest brother, and Paula was Tony's customer).

46

P.J told her that Tony was not home, and then she reached in and kissed him. He then explained how he stepped back and asked her what she's doing informing her of how he was in a relationship, but Paula did not care. Paula quickly responded with "I don't care I just want to Fu*k". From there P.J admitted that him and Paula had sex. How many hits can the heart endure before it shatters? We went back to his place. I didn't cry or show emotions, I was just quiet (which was highly unusual for me). While driving back I noticed everything. It's like I had sunk into myself but everything around me was magnified.

P.J looked very concerned after dropping the information on me, and while the piercing silence filled the car with a loud ring, I couldn't help but to scream on the inside. Once arriving to the house, we went straight to the back. P.J quickly grabbed me, held me, continuously kissed me, and we had sex. I didn't mind having sex, I didn't mind feeling anything other than the pain that was on me. Afterwards, I went to sleep, and he woke me up to deserts. While I was asleep, he picked us up some macaroons from my favorite bakery that he introduced me to. I looked up at him, said a quick but muffled thank you and laid back down. I didn't speak or say anything really until the next morning.

The next morning agony set in heavy. My mind kept asking questions. Kissing is one thing, but sex is another? Before him and Bella he had never cheated before, at least that's what was discussed whilst we were best friends. I had to break, the unknowing was killing me. So, I began asking him a bunch of questions about everything. How? Did you use protection? Was this something serious? I need to know because then I would know how to move.

In this process I didn't do what usual women would do. Women would usually stay away for weeks, even months, abstain from sex, or give their gentlemen the silent treatment. I did not step away nor push him away. No not any of that. All of that for me would be useless. For one he had already cheated, and I slept with him before knowing he cheated. Therefore, if I was to catch anything it would have already been transmitted. For two I knew I wasn't leaving him so why waste my time. Instead, I let him know how I felt and about my safety.

There was just too much going on at once, and with everything up in the air there was only two things I knew for sure. One I was in over my waist, and two; I was hurting. A few weeks passed by, and things went back to semi-normal. P.J promised he would never cheat again, and I believed him, but that did not remove the pain I was feeling. Picture going to a wellness clinic as a twenty almost twenty-one-year-old woman, asking to be checked for everything. The doctors' questions were intrusive and embarrassing, but hey I wanted to be a big girl, right. Although I was legally a woman, I felt as if I was still a child.

Truth be told I am considered a whole adult at this present day and time, but I still feel as if I'm just a big child with huge bills. "Ms. Mota why are you in for today?" that question rang in my ears like a doorbell. "Oh, doctor why don't you have a seat so I could drop some tea on you and tell you about how the one I gave my virginity too couldn't keep his jimmy in his pants. Or better yet the one-eyed snake was a little blind and bit the wrong girl. I wanted desperately to respond like this, but instead I responded and said I would like to be checked for everything please. Oh great !!! now I look like America's next top prostitute, I thought silently.

"Ms. Mota, how many partners do you have? Do you wear protection? When was the last time you had sex? Have you ever been pregnant"? Inquired the doctor. All of these questions were answered but with each one asked, I sank down more into myself. At the end of the questioning, I looked like a lost puppy to the female physician. Pathetic! Something I never wanted to look in front of anyone. What was worse was that I was there alone. I didn't tell him I was going to get checked. After all the silent worry my test came back clean and clear. Thank God!!! I thought to myself.

Yet I still felt as if I was leaving out with a disease. A condition better yet. A condition called "wondering". I wondered will things get better. I wondered will he wake up and see his best friend again. The one he basically promised to always love. With all the hurt that followed up the betrayal, this did not feel like love, but it filled me up like rocks in a bag; very heavy. The hurt went from crying about the situation to looking through Paula's and Bella's Facebook profile to understand what it was that I did not have. I never discussed this with him. I kept this part to myself. I Could have cheated on him, but I never even entertained another guy.

Every time someone (woman or male) showed interest or would try to talk to me, I would thank them for their compliments and let them know that I was in a relationship. I could understand if he cheated on me with his best friend or grew a sexual desire for someone that was always around; but the thought of him with some random female coming for a dime bag, not even dub, and sleeping with her unprotected, is what scared me the most. This type of hurt was different. Let me put emphasis on how random strangers and handsome ones at that, tried to speak to me, but I stayed loyal.

Hey, I was no Jennifer Lopez, but I was miles from an ugly duckling. I would always turn down offers. How could he? Why would he? How could he just so easily share something that should have only belonged to me? As these questions taunted me for weeks another tightrope situation occurred. A loved one of mines had moved north to make a better opportunity for her and her child. She lost transportation and where she relocated to everything was very far including workplaces. So, having a vehicle was a necessity After a conversation with my mom, I decided that I would eventually send up my car to help her and besides this would also get my mom off my back about who drove the car.

My mom did not want P.J driving the car because he was not on the car insurance. This caused for a lot of confusion because before my mom had given me her car it was P.J who was picking me up and taking me places. Even while we were just best friends, he took me everywhere when others could not. Which I found to be ironic because now I would be sending the car up more than four hours away to be driven by someone who was definitely not on the car insurance. This became an issue with P.J and I could understand his frustration but never knew that this would act as a catalyst for him to put a tight rein around my neck.

No job and no car spelt trouble. As the days progressed, I started giving odd names to certain days and learning quickly. Quickly of P. J's temper, and bad manners. Some days were beautiful, and some days were calf days. Calf days were the days, I walked on eggshells not to get him angry. Now that we are here let's dive right in. Let me get a little bit more specific about the calf days. About two or three weeks before giving up the car P.J and I had got into an argument about fish.

We were in our bedroom, P.J had just come from the front, and I had just got back from a day out. Immediately when I saw him, I ran and leaned into kiss him. I was always happy to see P.J. After The kiss P.J'S expression went completely empty. "Jalaina did you eat fish today", asked P.J. "Oh yes, I forgot". As I apologized, I quickly mentioned that I would go brush my teeth and gargle. Praying that he would not get upset; but that high hope subsided.

"How many times I have to tell you, don't kiss me if you eat fish. You are such a carnivore" replied P.J. As he continued to yell and scream at me, I turned to grab my bag in an attempt to go for a drive. This was really in efforts to allow things to cool down but before I could grab my car keys, he snatched up the keys ran outside, got in the car, and sped off. The way he put the car in reverse was as if he was going to go and crash the car. All I could remember saying was Lord in the name of Jesus. P.J quickly came circling back and sped up to the house. I saw a bunch of dust and the tires smelt like they were burnt.

P.J looked at me and said, "man you are lucky," while waiving his index finger. Ha something told me not to". After this, I hurried up and sent the car to my loved one's house, because if something was to have happened to it, I would not have been able to lie to my mom. After giving away the car, P.J was furious. I could understand his frustration because we needed the transportation, especially him because he was the one working, but I was tired of my mom calling about who was driving the car, as well as his reckless behavior with the car when upset. To ease the tenson I looked into getting a bike for myself. I did not want him taking me everywhere again, and when my father-figure heard that I gave the car away, he gave me a beautiful Beach cruiser to get around.

I loved the bike, and the seat was super comfortable. I named her "The Red Dragon". The bike came in quite handy, and with P.J covering the bills, I figured that I could at least ride my bike to school and utilize the bus whenever possible. P.J was the bread winner, and I must admit that this was a problem for me. However, I made sure to fulfill my duties as a woman, as well as helped with whatever I could to lighten the load. I never asked to get my nails, feet or hair done. I understood finances, plus with things like that I always took care of, or my momma took care of prior to me dating P.J.

I never really had to ask a man for things prior to me meeting him, so this was much different, and even with my efforts to lighten the load, P.J made my actions seem impossible at times. Once receiving my bike, things began to brighten up. A loved one of mines named Nettie hooked me up with a gentleman friend of hers that flipped houses. The gentleman was very intelligent. He would fix up houses, and have me clean them, so that he could rent them out. Mr. Charles had many houses. Nettie told me this would help keep a little cash in my pockets and that as a woman it was always important to have pocket cash.

Mr. Charles became fond of me, so he entrusted me with more responsibilities and taught me things like how to lay down pipes, and rid mold in houses. I loved learning about these things. Mr. Charles introduced me to his wife, child, and brother. He was very fond of his wife and was so respectful of me. I was very grateful for this opportunity and plus I thought that this would at least stop one of the areas that P.J would criticize me in. In P. J's words, "Jalaina, all you do is be around the house all day, if you're not in school." "I'm beginning to think you are a mooch".

Yeah, that's what it is, your nothing but a leech. Get up your fat f**k and do something". This is the way he would speak to me, and I was growing tired of it. Therefore, I found other alternatives of working. Not every job was paying decently or willing to work around my school schedule, and I was looking for something that would not be too rigorous while I was in med school.

So, I accepted side gigs, like filing and completing paperwork for older ladies, and etc. Although, I had my little side hustles, he continued utilizing the same nasty words towards me. As a matter of fact, these words became the usual when he was upset. It went from him calling me a leech to him calling me a fat bitch. There was one time he went as far as to tell me of how my friends turn him on more. This enraged me so much that I found myself calling him a small dick bastard, which in turn hurt his pride, but I stopped caring for that. I never really would go back in forth with him in the name calling, but I grew tired of him hitting me under my clothes.

I was stated by his size, besides he was the only size I ever had, but if I needed to defend myself in words, I would use that tactic. I wanted to hurt him the way he continuously hurt me. I wanted for him to have at least a clue of what he was doing to me as a woman emotionally. Besides that, I never just sat around. If I was not studying or going to school, I was cleaning, cooking, or helping him run errands. When he lost his license, I was the one who drove him everywhere to keep him from getting in trouble with the law. With him delivering marijuana to clientele, it was too risky without a license. So, I became his driver. I knew he was breaking the law; but if I could drive and help him it would ease my mind. Every time he took off, I worried.

I worried about his occupation and that he did not have a valid license. I did not like how this made me look. I remember crying one day after one of his clients noticed me and called my name. The young man could not believe his eyes. I cried after because this was not who I was or cared to be. Driving P.J around was like another job. P.J had a lot of clients, so we were always running. Some were doctors, lawyers, business owners, you name it. However, even with all my efforts his nasty comments towards me kept on coming.

To ease the comments and what I thought was the issue, I looked for work. For I thought work would change this idea of me being a leech, but it didn't. P.J found a way to cause trouble for me even in this area. One day while cleaning a two-story house for Mr. Charles, P.J called. "Jalaina why have you been there for so long?". I laughed and said I'm working. I thought he was a joke or something, because what else would I be doing other than working. With a cold response, P.J said I'm coming to get you." With a gentle sigh, I said okay let me call Mr. Charles and let him know that I have to leave. What P.J didn't know is that lot of times that I would be cleaning house for Mr. Charles he would be at others or running errands.

On this day Mr. Charles just so happen to be there. P.J zoomed up to the house, and Mr. Charles came out to greet him. Before leaving Mr. Charles and asked for a lift to another house that was further out, where his car was. I believe Mr. Charles did this to get more acquainted with P.J. With a devious grin P.J smiled and said sure. While Mr. Charles was in the car P.J was deliberately flying through the residential area. I was so embarrassed, and P.J had shown Mr. Charles the side of him that I was trying so hard to hide from my family. I thought I had lost my little job, but Mr. Charles loved me too much.

What I was most grateful for is that he did not out me to my loved ones. I thought it was because he was older, and that he understood. On the way home that day P.J was asking a series of questions. Like I had an affair on him or something. I quickly remind him that this was his forte not mines. Yes, I know you don't forgive a person for something, to turn around and to throw it in their face, but he was pushing it. That night he slept in his parent's place and left me alone. I hated this. I never wanted to go to bed angry. So, the next day I felt like I would make it up. This would be the day that I would stain our relationship. This day would serve as a new red flag and different level of rudeness exhorted from him. Early that morning I got up and jumped on my bike to ride to the nearest DD'S Discount.

It was not that near, but I wanted to purchase a few things, to surprise him. Upon purchasing shirts and a fly watch for him, I received a call. "Jalaina where are you?" I'm up the street, I will be home shortly. "No, I asked where you are?" he replied in a cold voice. I informed him that I was at DD's discount. "How did you get there?" "Uhm, I rode my bike". After a few moments of silence, he said that he would come to get me. P.J flew up in his brother's black car. Everyone shared cars around the family house. It was like a grab and go situation.

He got out the car, Snatched the bike from my hands and forced it in the back seat. As I looked at him in confusion, he said "get in"!! On the way to the house, I was hit with a serious of questions, like I was being dragged into custody. "DD'S is not close by what time did you leave?" "Seriously" I responded. As he bent the corners like we were fleeing the cops, I looked at him in utter confusion. "How did you get there so fast?" he asked.

"I told you already I rode my bike. "Look babe" I said to him calmly, "I went to get you some things, that's it". I lifted the bag up and smiled at him with hurt on my heart. From this, the questions had ceased, but his rageful look and reckless driving continued. Once we arrived, we went upstairs to his parent's part of the house. As P. J set on the couch and looked out the window, I walked over to hand him his things. "Look at some of the stuff I got you please", I hope you like it", I said in sincerity. One by one he pulled each item out, looked at it, and let it hit the floor. I did not get anything for myself, everything I brought was for him. Looking at him drop it on the floor, was discouraging.

Then his oldest brother Tony walked. Looking down at the bag of goods, Tony smiled and said "Oh snap this stuff is tight work, did Jamarra get this stuff for you? Dang, I wish my girl would do that for me". This made P.J very upset. Almost like a jealous upset. P.J grabbed up the stuff and went to put the bag in the closet. I swallowed my emotions and walked into the kitchen to cook. Whenever we cooked in his parent's part of the house we would make enough for the entire house. Although we were vegetarians, I could really cook, so I brought the flavor. P.J would always tell me how I brought flavor into his life. I figured cooking lunch/dinner would be a nice gesture to smoothen the coldness.

I made spaghetti, and this was one of his favorite dishes, so I just knew this would help. The smell alone was wonderful. Before I could pour out his plate. P. J came in the kitchen, looked over my shoulder and said, "what's this?" I said, "I'm cooking for us". When cooking vegetarian style substitute meat such as tofu, it is not easy unless it's by the brand called morning star. P.J began to argue with me about the food and how many packs were used.

But this time, I just didn't have it in me. I was not only tired but exhausted. "Listen eat it if you want". Before I could make my way out of his space to go into the office room, P.J picked up the entire pot, walked over to the window, and poured it out. As I watched in anger, I began to cry. P.J turned around and retorted, "What are you crying for? I can just buy some more". That right there is what became our problem. He would break things and hurt you, because he thought that he could simply buy it back. In disgust I turned away from him and ran down the stairs.

I was going to hop on my bike and get missing for the entire day, but whilst I threw my leg over to hope on my bike, he snatched it from under me. Catching my balance so that I would not fall, I turned back around to get my bike. "Where do you think you're going?", he asked. "Just give me my bike please." I responded, P.J dragged the bike to the side as I tussled to get it back from him, picked up one of the yard tools and started tearing and jagging holes in my bike tires. "Ride off now, and take your bike with you", he replied cynically. I then walked off and stayed gone for hours. P.J was blowing up my phone like the house burned down. How did I step into this and why haven't I stepped myself out of it? Why have I stayed? I asked myself.

Walking down the streets, in a not so safe area, I then responded back to myself, this is what I get for what I did to Bella. Walking down the streets I started to think, instead of hurting her, I believed I saved her. I actually saved her from all of this foolishness, she would have had to endure but stayed in for love. Either way I said to myself, you deserved this, Jalaina. I picked up my phone to the frantic but now humble P.J. Where are you? I'm worried, can I come to get you? Please, I'm sorry.

I don't know why I get like this", cried P.J. I told him no and that I would walk back shortly. What he didn't know is that I had an aunt in that area, and I wanted to keep it like that, just in case. I went to her house and sat with her for a couple of hours, before returning home. Upon coming up to the house, P.J was in the yard outside waiting for me. Look, I brought food for us and put the spare bed on the roof to fall asleep. I loved the weird gesture. This was part of the things that got me to stay. It wasn't the money; it was the tender weird loving things, because when it was good it was great, but when it was bad it was cold.

I loved the good days were the park days, Netflix nights, barn fires, and pitching a tent on the roof. I loved how P, J's house was huge, and it was great for climbing. P.J was also very earthy, so he created a garden with fruits, vegetables, and a beautiful acai berry tree. I helped him in the garden and that was my favorite as well. Where we would sit and eat acai berries together. These were the melancholy days. The days that would slightly drown out the pain of the bad. The bad days, when he would shove me out of the car to make me walk home, throw my things in the streets, and rip up my medical schoolbooks.

The good days somewhat sort of put water over the days where he would tell me that it was over or throw the fact of me not earning money and being heavier than I was in high school in my face. If we had opportunities to get on his friends' boat or have an extravagant adventure, he would remind me of how I should know it's a privilege for me to be there. The good days of him holding me in his arms and asking me to sing to him; drowned out the days when he would hit completely under the belt or refused to hold my hands in public; stating how we were not the relationship that he and Bella had.

Truth be told I never wanted to mimic them. I just wanted to love him in every way possible. I never cared about the money. I cared for him. When I believed things would mellow out, P. J's female cousin moved out and P. J's parents moved in two male relatives. One was P. J's uncle, and the other was his young cousin. This made P.J jealous, watchful, and territorial. As If was going to sleep with one of his relatives or something. I was a homemaker, and everyone could see that. Instead of P.J being proud of having a woman that knew how to cook, always cleaned, catered to him, and help him package up sales; he became jealous.

If someone was to truly give a complement or just try to have a mere conversation, it always ended up with him treating me like a cheap prostitute. What do I mean by this you ask? Let me tell you. On one fine day I was upstairs with his mom and his eldest brother. We were all talking and laughing…. just chilling. I loved his mom so much. Once I heard her story and what she had gone through in life; This made me respect and love her all the more. P.J walked upstairs with the coldest look on his face and juked his head beckoning me to follow him. I came downstairs and followed him to the backyard to inquire what was wrong. "Why were you upstairs talking with my brother so long?" I began to get leery of P. J's "why questions", because rage always followed.

After getting out of my head, I laughed and said "what?" I found it funny because, did he not see his mom up there as well? Once I perceived that it was not a joke, and that he was not playing, I became infuriated inside. "Hold on, for one it was me, your brother and your mom upstairs talking. Don't you ever disrespect me like this again. When you found me, I was untouched, not some bounced around whore.

What is your problem P.J? Like what is the actual problem?". "What's the problem, I will show you the problem" he retorted. P.J ran into our place and started dragging my things out of the house. Kicking some of my clothes and valuables that weren't in his hands. I watched as my underwear and clothes were hurled out of the door as he rushed back in so that he could take up our bed to throw it into the pool that he was digging up in the back yard. P. J's mom came out from hearing all the commotion. Calling out his full government name we both turned towards her. "Why are you doing this, is something wrong?"

What the hell is wrong with you?", yelled Mrs. Janie. My thoughts exactly, I thought to myself. P.J started cursing her out, and I intervened and said don't disrespect your mom like that. Looking puzzled, Mrs. Janie went marched to the front to call P. J's dad, while good ole Pee, flew into more rage. Running into the house, he went to grab my professional camera. I tried to get it from his hands, but it fell and hit the floor. While I pushed him back, he kicked at it and tried to rip the bag to get inside and smash the camera. I then completely snapped. This was something my mom brought me, and he was trying to tear it up.

"You want to play this crazy game. I'll show you crazy" I yelled. I had never gotten like this before, but I felt the color red. I left fighting for the camera and rushed inside for P. J'S things. I started throwing his clothes out of the drawers. "Don't worry all I have to do is fold them back, right baby!!", I yelled. P.J watched in shock. All the countless times he did this to me, I never responded in such a way. Ohh but this was a different day, he had finally taken me to a place that I tried to never go and that is petty.

In a burst of rage, I caught my breathe, glanced over at his precious Xbox, and began to help myself to it. "No!!!!, he yelled. "Yeah you want to tear up some stuff, buy this one back", I was shaking my head and throwing his stuff out like Madea. We began to fumble and out of nowhere Mr. Mason showed up. Mr. Mason was P. J's dad. "P.J what are you doing? Are you stupid?" asked Mr. Mason. "Pick this mess up now," he commanded but in a soft voice. Mr. Mason was never one to raise his voice. He was always reserved but swift. Mr. Mason looked over the year, and the down on the ground.

Where he saw my things, undergarments and etc. scattered over the back yard. His parents were unaware that this was going on, I always picked everything up well before. Besides it was never to that extent before either. As I was breathing heavily from the rampage that I embarked on as well, I couldn't help but feel embarrassed and stupid at the same time. Mr. Mason then put his head down almost like he was in shame and said, "I'm sorry for this Jamarra." After sincerely apologies went out Mr. Mason along with some relatives began to grab up some of my things. I begged them not to and that I could pick it up myself, but they quietly explained that it was okay and continued to help.

Together things were picked up in no time. A lot of things were salvageable, except for mattress that he threw inside the green-half - dug -out pool. It was very crazy to me how P.J calmed completely down. One thing I noticed was that P.J was extremely afraid of his dad. I don't care how much the beast barked in him, whenever Mr. Mason would show up, P.J would humble himself quickly. P.J helped to pick up everything and manicured the yard shortly after. Night came and like a puppy I was waiting around for my apology, a kiss, or some new trick out of a hat, so that we would make back up.

Our go to was not or never really make up sex, like most people get off on. P.J never had to beg/ask for sex. I never used it against him. But the whole pull something cool out of a hat (flattery) was common. So common that it became routine, almost like a restaurant's daily lunch special. I was slowly losing myself in a whole new way. I always told myself I would never let a man physically abuse me, but I learned that verbal abuse, manipulation and control was far worse. I had just about every form of abuse in life besides sexual, so I can state this with confidence.

A person can do far worse to an individual without putting their hands on them. Especially if your heart is connected. Emotional abuse tears at the heart and eats away at the mind. But hey that's another story for a different book. That night instead of going straight to sleep, I began to play in my head of the conversation that his mom and I had prior to me getting in the relationship with P.J. Ms. Janie was sitting on that white couch in the living room that was always decked out with exotic pillows. "Jamarra, I have been watching you," said Jainie. "Jamarra you are beautiful, smart, have everything going for yourself, and can have anyone you want". "Please don't fall for P.J.". As I was looking in disbelief and hurt for P.J; Mrs. Janie continued.

"My oldest son is a lot calmer and more settled", anyone but P.J". Justin would even make a fine match for you", said Janie. "Mrs. Janie why would you say such a thing about your son, when he would give the shirt off his back to help someone", I responded. "Because he is too much like his father" she replied. That was the last time Mrs. Janie ever commented on our relationship, apart from the night that should have broken the camel's back for me but didn't. I lay there and counted everything.

The jealousy, the rage, the control, the carelessness to my feelings and emotions. Just thinking of each made me grow a little more tired. I lay there unable to sleep as I had more flashbacks. Remembering a time when his jealousy, rage, and carelessness collided in one instant. On day his Jealousy and rage collided in one instant is when his sister, a group of friends, and I were getting ready to go out to the Brickell area. His sister was showering, and I was getting dress. The friends did not arrive yet. While getting dressed, I decided to dress a bit on edge, so that I would not stick out like a sore thumb.

Putting on my high-waisted jeans, with a black crop top Cami, I completed the look with an open cardigan. My hair was in plaits, so I put it over my shoulders and rocked some red lipstick. While exiting the room, his sister Mia took a long glance at me and smiled. Mia was always hip and into new fashions. "Oh, snap Jamarra you look good," said Mia. I smiled and humbly took her compliments. Getting ready to go outside, P.J. asked where I was going. looking me up and down. I smiled and said I'm going out with your sister babe. "No, you are not! Go change your clothes", said P.J. "Uhm I'm already dressed and yes, I am going out." P.J. grabbed my arm, and I snatched it back.

"What are you doing?", I said in disgust. We were outside in the bliss of day when P.J. began to grab at my cardigan in an attempt to rip it off me. I began to tussle with him in order to keep him from ripping my cardigan, but my efforts hailed to no avail. After successfully ripping off my cardigan, he started for the Cami bra. I went from begging him to stop to tussling and holding my clothes to me. Every time I asked him to stop, that strengthened him to be even more outrageous. I was more concerned of being exposed, because we were in the front yard.

While he was able to rip one arm strap off of the Cami, I made my way for the house. I knew that if the top had ripped completely off my breast would have been exposed. I believe that was the only thing that kept me from fist-fighting him. The fact of not bearing my breast to the neighborhood. So, my aim was just to get into the house, while P. J's motives were entirely different. In the final attempt, I used my body weight. This made me in the house, and into his sister's room. The light back cardigan that connected towards the bottom, and my beautiful Cami was destroyed.

On that night I didn't even want to touch or look at him. I remembered feeling like Cinderella, when she initially spent all her time cleaning and making a beautiful dress, for only her jealous stepsisters to rip it off her just before the major event. Even with this cruelty, there was no apology given. Instead, he spoke to me while thought I was asleep to say. "You just don't know how beautiful you are Jalaina". I heard him but never responded. I was too hurt. As I had snapped back to reality, I realized how everything was hurting. We slept in the same bed, and he cuddled me. I wouldn't deny him that, but I showed no emotion.

It's like something in me almost turned off that night. As he held me close the flashbacks started pouring in. Flashbacks that were bitter without the sweet. In that instant and moment, I realized if I was to count everything, and write a recollection of everything bad, it would certainly drown out the good times and I would run out of paper. Several weeks went by, and we made up and did our daily things that would usually help time pass. Then on a Sunday morning P.J. and I went to visit a church with my church community. Upon leaving out of the church, there was this long patio stool that was shaded by a wonderfully shaped tree.

As I was admiring the splendor of the tree, P.J. grabbed my hands and walked me over to the stool. "Please sit down for a moment, I need to ask you something" he calmly asked. When I sat down P.J. kneeled and said, "Jalaina will you marry me". I looked at him to take in the moment and then I immediately said, "Yes, and yes again". The day was well spent as I pondered on the fact of how we were now engaged to one another. From news such as this, one would think a girl would have alerted Channel 7 news, but this was not the case.

I did not tell anyone, friends, or family. Instead, I kept quiet to let everything settle in. The next day, P.J. proposed to me again, asking for my hand in marriage. At first, I laughed it off, but when I saw how serious he was, I gave him a calm and sincere reply. "Babe, I already said yes. My feelings haven't changed". P.J. responded, "I know, but I haven't proposed with the ring yet." I told him that whether the ring came from a store or a bubble gum machine, it wouldn't change the fact that I loved him, and my answer was still yes. I kissed him a few times and wrapped my arms around him to show him that I really meant it.

I wanted P.J. to understand that the diamond didn't matter to me as much as the commitment did. In my eyes, we were already engaged, and anything man-made was just material. Despite my assurances, P.J. asked me two more times before the final proposal with the ring. The last attempt would have been executed with the ring, but it was not carried out. The last time was never executed because the last straw that broke the camel's back was finally drawn. Truth be told breaking was already set in motion with several occasions of painful days and nights. Occasions where I should have left the relationship but stayed.

The night that should have broken the camel's back but didn't was an extremely hurtful one. This night served as a new marker of total disrespect and another level of rage. When in a relationship such as this, there are markers to every level, in which is imperative to know, but I was not enlightened until the very end. Information was being acquired while I endured through every experience, and what I gathered was how emotional abuse could also pour over into physical abuse if allowed. However, this factor solely depends on the individuals involved.

Not to mention, this type of abuse could go on longer than physical as well as unnoticed because of people's ignorance to the power of words and the lack of physical scars. Words have the power to break an individual, cutting them to their very soul, making emotional abuse to be a silent killer. Physical abuse breaks down the body while emotional deals with the psyche but when words and then actions collide you have something entirely different. Now the night that should have broken the camel's back but didn't, truly started in the daytime and was carried into the night.

During the day things were already not so light. P.J was aggie and there were some heavy family situations transpiring, on top of this my mother had brought her Dachshund over for P.J and I to keep for a few days while her patio was being properly fumigated. That night while sitting down and chilling with the dog my best friend Ivan called. Ivan was my childhood best friend, but after a while his family moved and him and I were only able to spend time occasionally because of distance. Once Ivan was older, he would catch the train to come and spend time with me but then after high school he enlisted in the army. Therefore, the chances of really seeing him were slim to none.

When my phone lit up with an out of area number my heart burst for joy. I just knew it was Ivan. Receiving phone calls were rare simply because of where he was stationed and his everyday duties, but he sent letters to our entire friend group. I put the dog down, grabbed up my phone and answered it. "Hey Jalaina" Ivan yelled out in excitement. Before I could respond P.J. grabbed my phone and threw it across the room. My cellular went three separate ways. The front, back and battery. I lost the call. From this I gave him a look that would make your skin curl. "Why would you do this" I asked. Before he could answer I gave the truth.

"You can't stand the fact of me even speaking to another male, but you have a girl best friend. Not to mention the fact that you cheated on me with your brother's client who you later picked up as a client and would still be dropping dimes off too had I not checked you". "Don't you ever do that again". P.J said not a word but went over to the corner where my phone was and began stepping on it and smashing it with his feet. "Yeah, I'm not doing this I'm leaving". The usual M.O for P.J was to destroy my stuff and yell how we were over. I never told him that I would leave before and when I said this, I truly meant that I would leave the house for the moment not him in general.

"You want to leave". I ran and grabbed my bag and dashed for the dog but unfortunately, for Nikko P.J grabbed him up quick. "You want to leave, he said with a nasty demeanor go, leave Jalaina." While he held the dog with aggression, I spoke calmly to de-escalate the situation. "Just give me the dog please". P. J's uncle was there that night and came out from his room. "P.J you need to stop this. I have been watching you, and how you treat her, and you're going to regret it.

You have a beautiful young lady who cares for you and if you do not change these ways, you are going to lose. I never interfered before, but this is disgraceful" he cried out. "You are now becoming a disgrace to our family line of man". "You have stopped wearing deodorant, you are completely disrespectful, and on top of this you have been smoking day in and day out you like something is wrong with you". "Mind your own business uncle I never get into the matters you have with your women, so stay out of mine" P.J replied.

His uncle screamed out in a very authoritative tone "Give the young lady back the dog!!! or I'm calling Mason. Mr. Tazz threats of calling P. J'S father made him become even more outrageous. Instead of handing me back the dog, P.J ran out the door and climbed to the roof with the dog. "You want to leave Jalaina, go ahead and leave!!!". As he yelled from the roof top, he also dangled the dog over by its neck. Little Nikon began to screech as I began to beg and cry "please bring him down, I'll stay". With tears in my eyes, I continued to beg, but P.J squeezed Nikon's neck a little bit more. Mr. Mason pulled up and Mrs. Janie jumped out the car.

"P. J what the hell are you doing", babe look at your son" yelled Janie. Mr. Mason went to the roof and was able to retrieve the dog and the fiancé. Mr. Mason walked over to bring Nikon to me as well as instruct me to call my mom and return the dog. He did not have to inform me of this, because that was the first thing on my mind. As I was grabbing the dog from Mr. Mason Mrs. Janie looked over, waltz up to me and clapped in front of my face. "Wake up" " wake up Jamarra" yelled Mrs. Janie. "Why are you yelling at the girl like that Jane," said Mr. Mason. "Because she needs to wake up babe" replied Mrs. Janie.

Grabbing the dog up again, Mr. Mason calmly said "The dog will stay with us for tonight, Jamarra, but first thing in the morning he has to go". "Okay, will do, and thank you Mr. Mason" I responded. I sat at the front steps of the house, wondering how I could have done things differently, while P.J came up and looked at me almost like he was disgusted with me. Pulling out his penis he began to urinate in the flower bush that set over from the step of his parent's door while yet directly in front of me.

I said nothing, but P.J then went to continue to pee from the bush to the ground near my feet. As almost if he wanted to pee on my feet but reframed himself. He had made a line with his piss by my feet, like drawing in the sand, so close that I received the back splatter from the ground onto my feet. As he completed his horrible task, I looked up and said this is called mental abuse. "This is what this is". As I said this out loud, I was really talking to myself. I had just caught the epiphany that night. P.J looked at me, shook, then tucked himself and pulled out his phone to call my mom.

When I gathered what he was doing I begged him not to, but it was too late she had answered. I did not want any of my loved ones to know what was going on because little did, he know, they would have killed him. "Hello Ms. Janie, I'm calling to say that maybe you need to come pick up your daughter. She feels as if she is being mentally abused, and I don't want to abuse her so come get her". In a very arrogant and careless voice, P.J exposed himself and a small bit of his character. That night as we laid down, I forced myself to sleep. I was upset, broken, and in disbelief of the monster I was laying next too. Where was the one that would kiss me softly? The one who would have water fights with me?

The one who allowed me to drive for my very first time on the expressway? The one that took me to different dessert places that I had never been to because he knew how much I loved sweets? Where was my sweet, playful, goofy love? Why was it just me now? Yes, I did not have a full-time job, yes, I understood the pressure, but if the tables were turned, I would have done the same for him but more. I would have never thrown it in his face neither mistreated him because of it. I was doing things for him that I would never do for anyone. How was it that he could not see this love.

In the morning, I woke up before he could. I put clothes on and ran out of the house barefoot into the grass. Him and I lived in the back where we had our own entrance along with his two other relatives. How I hope that the there was no gate in the back yard and just field, because I would have kept running. I remember the feel of the fresh lightly wet grass and the early morning sun kissing my face. The birds in the distance singing their usual tune and the huge tree that surrounded their large gate in the back. For that moment I could feel and remember in that instant when I once felt safe. When I once felt safe, was in middle school; it was just me and my mom living together.

My brother and sister were not living in the house and my mom had not yet met her fiancé. The house was so peaceful, and my mother and I would go to church every Sunday with my second mom. My second mom was my mother's best friend that claimed me as her own from when I was a little one. She would always tell me of how when my mother had me, she told her "This one is mines". There were some years as a child where I felt safe but not so much because I underwent sibling abuse.

I know people say brothers and sisters' fight, yes, but our fights were different. Much different, but hey that's an ole bag of bones for another dog to lick. I went on to remember the time where I was going to church with my mom every Sunday, where I was in school at the top of my class. Unbothered, untouched, and free. This was a time I felt most safe. From this feeling, I looked back at our front door, turned around and ran up the tree. I went up and set up high so that I could think for a while and ponder on everything. The good, the bad and the in- between. As I was thinking I heard P. J's voice calling my name.

"Jalaina, Jalaina!! I scooched back further in the tree and watched him walk around the house to look for me. I said nothing. "Jalaina, Jalaina!!" For once it felt good not to answer or jump to his beck and call. Before he could yell out my name again, I answered, "Yes, I am here." "Here, where?" yelled P.J. As I climbed down the tree, he looked at me for a while and then grabbed me by the hands to lead me up the steps. We both sat down with him directly behind me and I did not know what to expect. "You can't leave me. I don't have no one, I can only trust you. I can't live without you" he stated. Some women think that this is sweet and complimenting.

However, this is no compliment. This is a warning depending on whose mouth its coming from. I was worried and concerned for him, and although I wasn't thinking of leaving, I kept this saying close to heart. I knew was time to leave him, but I didn't want to. My heart wouldn't be able to. I was in love but in the same sense felt stuck like a cat in a river. My mom pulled up in that blue box car, to pick up Niko and demanded that I get in the car also. "Okay let's go", said mom. "No, I'm staying here mom." "No, you're not either your coming home", said mom.

"Listen I love him, and he is my first, I'm staying", I retorted". "Jalaina that does not matter, please get in this car" begged mom. "No momma I'm staying", I so hurtfully replied. I knew what would be best, but if I left, I would be leaving my heart also. Mom looked at me with hurt, regret, disbelief, and most of all, similarity. It's like she was looking at herself in me. As if she knew the look on my face; she had seen it years before on her. The look that said, I know it's time to go but I'm too far lost to leave. That day was rather calm afterwards. I went to the back where P.J and I resided to clean, shower and then lay down. P.J came to the back cuddled me and we fell asleep. In the middle of the night P.J woke me up.

"You are not real", he said with a serious countenance. "You are not real; this is not real" repeated P.J. I signed, shook my head, and then told him "Yes, it is, I love you, and I'm staying". I held him closer, and we both went to sleep. I later understood it was not that he was calling me fake, but it was the fact that with everything we went through, I still stayed. The next day my mom called P.J and asked him if he and I would move into the house. Mom claimed that she was moving out and in with her fiancé, and that my brother was not cleaning but tearing up the house instead. After their conversation P.J came to me to have the discussion.

"Jalaina we are moving out of my parents' house and moving into your mom's. P.J. wasn't asking me but more so demanding it. "No, we are not" I quickly replied. 'Then we are over" he said. "Ok, well I guess we will be moving in at my mother's house". I smiled on the inside; Yeah, we will move in alright, when the rat gets a national holiday. After two or more weeks P.J caught my drift. He wasn't at all an idiot; he was quite intelligent. So, the fight began. He intentionally started an argument with me, told me we were over, and started packing my things in his car. I did not have a lot to pack considering that he tore up most of my things in previous disputes. On the car ride over to my moms, I did not ask no questions. When we pulled into the driveway of my mom's house, my brother came out to get my things". "Welcome home sis". "He was welcoming me home while my mind was on P.J." My mother was no longer living at the house, she had in fact moved in with her fiancé. I walked into a house that was very cluttered.

My mother had purchased so many things that there were multiple living room sets. She always had exquisite taste and appreciated a good shopping experience, but this was different. She was over-purchasing, and it wasn't like her. As I tried to come up with a game plan to get the house organized and clean, I started asking myself how and when things got into these conditions. I spent time with her, but never at the house, so I didn't notice it happening. After an incident where a loved one trashed the house, I didn't really spend much time there. I remembered P.J and I picking up glass piece that were shattered over the ground as well as everything else.

We stayed at her house for maybe a day or two to make sure she was safe, but after that, I never really came back. I was so wrapped up in helping P.J. with his deliveries that I neglected other things. I had fallen in love and into assisting foolishness. My fiancé lived a life very different from mine, but I was submerged into his. That day at the house, my brother was curious about what was happening with my relationship, and of course, I took the blame for everything. Night had arrived and P.J. came to the house apologizing and stating that that he did not want to break up with me. However, he conveniently already had all of his things when he showed up.

I understood that the entire charade he pitched during that morning was to ensure that we moved into my mother's home. However, I did not argue with him, but opened the door and helped him with his things instead. That night we cleared out a room so that we would have somewhere to lay our heads for that night. I refused to live in the house in the condition it was in, so I began to formulate a plan of how I would organize and make sense of everything. Some days had passed, and my mother moved my two girl best friends in. Things were seemingly okay for a while.

I began to become hopeful because things were quite better than the emotional abuse that I was subject to while living with him at his parents' house. However, this hope was short-lived. My brother had taken off, so it was just myself and the girls. Then one day P.J. and I got into a disagreement where he broke maybe one or two glass pot tops in the house and flew out the door. I tried to clean everything up before the girls could witness it, but that was to no avail. As I was picking up the mess, the girls were looking concerned while trying to speak with me about him and what I should do. Everything they were saying was for my good, but I didn't care to listen.

Well, the truth was at the time I didn't want anyone talking to me, I just wanted someone to help me clean up the mess. I was breaking all over and I just needed someone to pass me -the glue. One of the girls became frustrated "I'm done talking, I will tell your mom about what happened here today," said Diamond. I became infuriated at Diamond's remarks, and I found myself asking both to leave. "What" the girls replied, "Jaliana you can't be serious". "Yes, I'm serious please get out," I said. I hurt them and I didn't mean to. I didn't mean for anyone to get hurt, not even me. Later on, everyone had come back, and things went back to normal, but the girls were not touching on the issue or the topic anymore. Days had passed and together the girls and I had set the house up very nicely. P.J. threw in some assistance as well whenever he could. I moved everything around and utilized one room as storage: filling up that room with my mother's belongings. Once the house became hospitable, mom started purchasing more things to bring. "It's as if she said, oh look, I have more space". A few months later, P.J.'s family and I went to Puerto Rico. P.J. covered all my expenses for the trip. It was my first time traveling out of the country. For the entire week, we stayed in the mountains near old San Juan, and it was incredibly beautiful.

There were horses, mountains, butterflies, waterfalls, and more. Unfortunately, my menstrual cycle started, and it made me extremely sick for two days. One of those days was when we had planned to go ziplining. I told P.J. to go without me, but he insisted on staying with me. I didn't want him to miss out because of me, but he refused to leave my side. Everyone left and it was just him and I in the cabin. Maybe an hour or so in, P.J. asked for us to go to the waterfall that we had hiked to earlier in the week. "I would love to babe, but I don't feel well", "I apologize but this will not be possible".

Utilizing this as a means to start an argument, P.J. went back and forth with me about how the waterfall was nearby. When I said that I couldn't, he eventually blurted out his frustration about missing the ziplining experience. "I told you to leave, and that I would be fine here in the cabin," I said as I tried to reason with him. The argument continued as we exchanged hurtful words. Before I could try to calm the situation, P.J. took my ibuprofen and poured the entire bottle of medicine across the cabin floor. This upset me because I would have to search for the pills on the wooded cabin floor, and he knew how much pain my menstruation brought me every month. Before I knew it, the worst words left my mouth. "I hate you" I shouted. P.J. grabbed my clothes that were in the suitcase and tossed some of my items over the hill. "With everything you have done for me, you mess it up with your actions. I screamed at him as he was emptied my clothes from the suitcase. The work you put in with your hands you mess up with your feet" I yelled. "You hate me, Jaliana!" he cried out. Instead of answering, I cut my eyes and turned around to go in the room. "Have fun being stupid by yourself" I retorted.

That night was no lovely dovie situation. Words were not taken back either. I loved P.J. more than I could ever express. I did not hate him, but something was brewing on the inside. I didn't know if it was regret, I didn't know if it was anger or rage, but there was a new feeling springing forth. Maybe it was a combination of everything combined. Two things I was completely sure of were that I felt a lot of hurt and that it began to choke out the good. The next morning, we were at each other's throats again. I pushed him and he pushed me back. Mrs. Janie, P. J's relatives, and the so-called "Other wife" came out to break us up.

The "Other Wife" is a long story for someone else to tell of how lust won but love still stayed. There are so many faces to the word love. "You think you're so smart, but guess what Jalaina, they kicked you out of the medical program". shouted P.J. "They sent a letter before the trip, but I didn't tell you, I was going to speak to you after the trip". The bad news rang in my ears like a nagging alarm that set to wake you up in the morning. Mrs. Janie saw my face and advised for me to toughen up. "With this family you will need". I didn't utter a word the entire day. I was in such a beautiful place but very ready to go back home.

76

Later, in the afternoon, P.J came to speak to me and apologize. I accepted the apology, but I didn't want to see tricks out of the hat, if it would have been a rabbit that he pulled from behind his back, I would have shot it. Again, tricks out of the hat would be taking me places I have never been, bringing back deserts that I would like, etc. P.J caught my drift of how I was feeling, and he wouldn't come near me. I appreciated that. The next day, we went on a trip further up the mountain and met a couple who were farmers.

The wife showed us something amazing called miracle fruit. It was a small seed that you suck on, and after doing so, anything sour you put in your mouth afterward would taste super sweet. As we drove back down the mountain, I remembered asking God a serious question: "Lord, I love this man so much, why does he hurt me so much?" I heard a response: "Why do you hurt me so much?" I never asked that question again. This was the most important answer I could ever get back that would serve me for life. When God answers, his response never dies. We are created in God's image and his likeness.

We, as individual beings, never take into perspective that God has emotions and feelings just like we do. So, when we sin and are disobedient, this hurts him as well. I thought about how we have a Father who loves us unconditionally, we never really lay down and truly reverence him in the way that we should. We hurt Abba daily. God's response was so profound that it woke up something inside me. When we returned to the United States, I continued working at my mom's house. P.J. was at the house whenever he could, because he still had a line of work to do, but it wasn't going to happen at my mom's house (I made that clear).

We had a few rough days, but it was still smoother between us at my mom's house than at his parents' place. Everything was going okay until it wasn't. One day, my best friend and I were in the bathroom together. She was taking a shower, and I was using the toilet when P.J. called. "Where are you?" he asked. "In the bathroom with Lisa, is everything okay?" I replied. "I just don't understand why you have to take showers together," P.J. scolded. "It's just something we do, something we've done for years," I quickly replied. "Well, no wife of mine is going to be taking showers with another woman, that's disgusting," P.J. replied. At that moment, I could feel my blood boiling.

"No wife of yours could ever do anything. I have sacrificed a lot of things, but what I do with Lisa is off-limits. Everything else is dictated, but not this," I responded authoritatively. I was tired of the "no wife of mine" comments when we weren't even married yet. There were many instances where I could have given ultimatums, but I didn't. I didn't want my future husband to sell marijuana, go natural and refuse to wear deodorant, yell at me, call me names, tear me down, and then come back and apologize. I certainly didn't want a husband who would ask me to consider a polygamous marriage.

I was tired of the disrespect, the rage, and the ultimatums. I wasn't even showering with her that day; I was on the toilet. I could have said that, but I wanted to make it clear that I wouldn't stand for anything else to be taken from or commanded of me through an ultimatum as ridiculous as no wife of mine. Especially since we weren't married yet and proposal or not, no more ultimatums. When I refused his request, P.J. threw a tantrum. He yelled, "I'll come get my stuff, move out, and we're over!" before hanging up the phone.

I didn't want him to cause a scene, especially with Lisa there, so I quickly finished up and washed my hands to go to the front. When I got there, I saw that he had already been there. I realized that he had come into the house, noticed we were in the same bathroom, called my phone to give the ultimatum, and then stormed out, leaving the door wide open. Feeling frustrated, I locked the door and headed to the room. After a few minutes, P.J. came back. Flying up in the driveway, jumping out of the car, and storming through the door like he had caught me in the act of adultery.

"Pee, can we just sit down like rational human beings and discuss this through?" I asked calmly. As he slammed our bedroom dressers to grab his clothes to pack them up. I stopped him "Listen we not doing this in my mom's house. You would not do this in your parents' part of the house because Mr. Mason would knock your head off, so don't do it here". When I said this P.J. became furious. He ran to the closet where I stored the gifts. I had saved up money from cleaning houses to buy Christmas gifts for everyone. He snatched each out and threw it across the room. I watched as boxes were launched across the room. Every makeup set, glass figurine, pocket purse, and toy I scanned as it hit the floor.

Before I knew it, I snapped. I grabbed him by the shirt and slung him out of the room. P.J. rushed back in and pushed me down. I jumped up with my fist closed tight. Apart from me wanted to punch him so hard that his mother would feel a contraction. I believe God told me not to punch him, and besides I put my hands on him first. Instead, I asked him to leave. He quickly refused. "If you do not leave, I will call the cops" I retorted. I wasn't going to call the authorities on him, but I just said that to get him to leave.

Instead of leaving, he flew into a frenzy, went outside picked up a few flowerpots, and hurled them at the house. Trying to look where the noise was coming from and where all the pots were landing, P.J. then opened our bedroom window, stuck the water hose inside, and turned it on. I ran outside and turned the water off. Meanwhile, P.J. sped off. In my heart, I was just tired. I needed respect. After cleaning up the mess that Mr.'s temper tantrum had created, I went next door to my neighbors to sit and ponder.

Will he ever respect me? I have sacrificed everything that I could to show my love. Even with the conviction of pre-marital sex, sitting with the pastor and P.J., dealing with the embarrassment, and mom's new way of treatment against me after losing my virginity. With all of this sacrifice, no respect was given to me on his part. I sat and waited for his call. I knew he would be calling to apologize and just like clockwork, I received the call. This time around would be different. I was going to make it different. On the phone, I remembered him saying "Jalaina I apologize, and I know that I need to work on how I respond to things.

I just really love you and we could also work on things". "Babe, I understand that, and I do forgive you, but this is all the time, I believe we need to take a break". I calmly replied. I let him know that the break wouldn't change anything and that I was still in love with him. I placed my rules on the table. For one I was going celibate, for two no more shacking with one another. We would still be in a relationship but would no longer live together or have sex until we were married. P.J began to beg, promising that he would get help and change. I believed him, but I was tired of sacrificing and going against God and my morals, only to end up getting the short end of the stick. So, I called for the very first break.

In four years, I had never set limits like this before. The only boundary I had set from the beginning was that no man would ever lay their hands on me. I refused to be a victim of physical abuse. Looking back, I was at a point where I was trying to figure out which was worse: physical or mental and emotional abuse?

CHAPTER EIGHT

Obedience is Better!

The first few days of the break felt like I was passing a kidney. I called him, but he did not answer. I cried every night, feeling like someone had cut out a huge chunk of my heart. I visited his parents' house when I could, but he was not there most of the time. Still, I made sure to cook whenever I could. I started praying more and speaking to prophets about the situation, so that I could pray for both him and me. I prayed so hard that one day, while I was on the bus coming from school, P.J. called me. "Jalaina, I know you're praying for me, I hear you! Stop!" said P.J.

I smiled, and this just made me pray even more. I was convinced that he was coming back as prophesied, and I was going to have him back.Several days had passed, as I went through the turmoil of separation. I remember sitting on the couch by the window one day, praying, when I heard God say, "He will propose to you in December." I was confused because P.J. had already proposed to me, and I had said yes. Then the Lord said, "This time it will be with the ring." I thought, "Perfect, I will say yes." But the Lord replied, "No, you will not, because by this time you will not be together."

I got up, rebuking the devil. One afternoon, I went to P.J.'s house to spend time with him but ended up speaking to Mrs. Janie instead. I remember there was a day I was sitting on the couch by the window. I was praying and then I heard God say, "he will propose to you in December." I was confused, and I said to myself this can't be the

Lord speaking to me, because P.J. had already proposed to me, and I said yes. The Lord said, "This time will be with the ring". "I said perfect I will say yes". The Lord replied, "No you will not, because by this time you will not be together". I got up rebuking the devil. One afternoon I went to P. J's house to spend time and see him, when I ended up speaking to Mrs. Janie instead. I found out that even though she was the one telling me to wake up, Mrs. Janie sounded as if she was on his side. "Jamarra, why have you separated from P.J., and stopped having relations?" she asked.

I told Mrs. Janie that I wasn't separating myself from P.J. and I loved him tremendously, but I was waiting for marriage to live with him. I explained to her that I wanted to completely change my life and rededicate myself to God. "Yes, I understand that but P.J. already bought you a ring, it's in the safe, what is this all about, what more do you want?" Looking her straight in the eyes, completely baffled, I said nothing. I was baffled because she confirmed the ring and what I heard that day on the couch as I was praying. This left me tongue-tied. "I'm waiting and trying to do things the correct way," I retorted.

After our conversation, I picked up my things and went back home. The separation was hard. I remember thinking of him night and day until a loved one called me. "Jalaina, can I ask you a question?" said the prophet. "Yes. Yes, you may," I replied. "Who was the first person you thought of when you woke up?" he asked. "P.J.," I quickly responded. "Okay when you went to sleep, who did you think of?". "I thought of P.J." I responded. "That is called idolization, the Lord is leading you to go on a fast. For the next three days don't call, respond to, or text P.J. For the next three days he will be calling you like crazy but don't answer" he instructed. I truly found that hard to believe because he wasn't calling me at all.

Nonetheless, for the next couple of days, I fasted and sought the Lord; while P.J. called like he was losing his everlasting mind. The minute I got off the fast I called him, and he wouldn't answer. I called for days with no answer. So, one day I decided to go over to his. I felt in my spirit not to go to his house, I knew the Lord told me not to, but I wanted to see him, smell him, and hug him. I just wanted to be around him. When I reached his house and he saw me, we took to one another. I missed him so much and I truly wanted to see him. The entire day he behaved himself as the perfect gentleman. Until he wasn't.

I was quite sure we would be back together and push forward the engagement to marriage, but the things that would unfold that night would put a damper on the very thought of the union. The day was well spent, and it was time for P.J. to take me home. Before dropping me home, P.J. informed me that he had to make a quick stop at his friend's house to drop something off. When we arrived, Harold ran out with a smile to the car. At the window, he came up to P.J. and yelled, "Did you do it? Harold was asking P.J. basically if he proposed with the ring. I looked over at P.J. and his entire mood was down,

I had to take a second look because it was as if the young man that I had known for years was unrecognizable in that instant. I turned my head around stared at the dashboard and started questioning God. "God, will I make it home tonight?" P.J. responded to Harold with a no and maybe another time. "Okay, well man I'm sorry about that" replied Harold clapping P.J. up. As we drove off from Harold's P.J.'s demeanor was different, and he was stone quiet for the ride up. Everything felt different, so I knew not to ask any questions or start a conversation. Instead,

I watched the streets as we headed up to my house. Once we were about three minutes away from the house, P.J. turned off, made a right turn, and headed to the expressway. Despite having to pass through three major traffic lights, we still miraculously made it to the expressway in under 3 minutes. "Where are you taking me?" Can you please slow down?" I asked. P.J. was flying on the expressway, weaving through the traffic. I knew in my spirit that he was aiming to hurt me. I knew he was aiming to hurt him and me. "Slow down, please, you're going too fast" think about our lives P.J."

I screamed. "Fuck our lives, you used me. You and your mom" he retorted. "Wait a minute I sacrificed everything, and I used you? You had an entire affair; can you just please slow down and take me home" I begged. P.J. continued to drift through the traffic. "I'm not going to let you kill me, you won't get that opportunity" I replied. I tried to get the car door open, but it was so hard to get it open because he was speeding. Once I was able to get it at an angle to jump out, P.J. snatched me back in, slammed on brakes, went towards the dashboard, and fell completely upright in the seat. "Oh my God what was I going to do," said P.J. as he began to cry.

In utter disbelief, acknowledging that he was trying to hurt us, I rubbed his shoulder and said it's okay you could just take me home. "I'm not taking you home !!!!". He looked at me and then back at the road and bolted off. He was speeding again and not in the fun adrenaline rush way, but in an unmanageable and out of control way he went full speed ahead. The road to the expressway was looping for a turn but he was going straight. I heard the Lord say for me to call prophet. At the time, I said to myself I could not call prophet, that it was too late, and he was married. The Lord said again to me, "Call prophet".

So, I called and surprisingly at 2 am, he answered. The prophet spoke to him to calm him down. "Pee I know you love Jalaina, but this is not the way to go about things" He then began to say other things that which I tuned out because I was trying to think of ways to escape without Jumping out of a car. Jumping out of a car that was going more than 110mph on the expressway was no longer the idea, nor was it befitting. "Jalaina". The mention of my name snapped me back to reality "Jalaina" said the prophet. "Yes", I replied. "Call me when you get home," he said. I responded and said okay, but deep down I didn't believe I would be making it home that night.

I always wondered how I would die imagining the many different scenarios, but at the hands of someone I deeply loved was not something that ever crossed my mind. P.J. drove us out far north. When we got off on an exit, he slowed down completely. I saw an officer at a service station and turned my head to the window. P.J. took one sharp look at me and said if you dare. I turned from him and wiped my face. P.J. pulled to the side of the road and started talking. He spoke at me for a long time while I stayed quiet. I refused to speak to him. He then turned the car back on and headed back.

P.J. took us to his parent's place, it had to be perhaps thirty minutes past three close to four a.m. in the morning. I got out of the car and walked into his parent's part of the house and then up the stairs. P.J. was directly behind me. I ran into his parents' room. Mr. Mason and Mrs. Janie were startled. "Jamarra is everything okay" they asked. My heart was racing. I looked to my right and saw P.J. at the door looking just like how he looked before taking off from Harold's house. Cold, dangerous, and not himself. "Nothing, I just wanted to say Hi" I replied in a faint voice.

"Goodnight you guys," I said just before closing their door. Letting out a schmuck laugh, P.J. said, "You are very, very smart, for what I would have done you wouldn't have liked it." I walked into the office room with P.J. He had me lie down so that he could hold me. Something inside of me knew that if I had taken the other route of escape with his parents it would not have ended well for me. It's like the Lord led me that night with what to do and how to move. The same way he led me the night when this young man was trying to attack me years before.

I had to fight and discern my way out of that one, just like I had to listen and discern my way out of this night. I remembered that voice, so I listened. In the morning P.J. woke up with a smile on his face. I mean he grinned like a kid who was awarded the big rainbow lollipops from the dollar store, versus a young man who had just kidnapped a whole human being and forced her to lay down with him to cuddle. "See that's all I wanted to do" "I just wanted to hold you," he said proudly. In my head I thought, wow all he wanted to do was cuddle Jalaina. So, with him seeming like he wanted to run us off the bridge last night was just the bonuses of cuddling; oh boy.

P.J. snapped me out of my inner thoughts when he commented "Now I will take you home". Once I arrived home, I remembered walking through the door of my mom's house. I should have praised the Lord but all I could think of was how? I remember thinking that he dropped me off but all the trust that I had for him was left behind on the bridge where he completely lost his cool. I loved him but I lost every bit of trust, and I would soon find out just how important trust was to me. In life, because we walk in our bodies, and understand our traits, colors like, and dislikes; we somehow believe that we have ourselves figured out.

However, the actual truth of the matter is that we don't even know ourselves fully. Once placed in unprecedented circumstances or experiences, is when you find out who you truly are. To be specific, I never knew that I would fall in love so young. I never knew that I would lose my virginity at the young age of 20. I mean yes, I played around before in the past with kissing and some other basses but never the actual thing. I never knew that I would be involved in a mentally abusive situation. I suffered physical abuse as a child from siblings, but mental abuse is far worse, especially from the one that you would have crossed an ocean for and with.

I remember years back P.J. asked me if I would move somewhere completely new and away from everyone that we knew. My answer was yes, and when? Could he not see my love? As if I did not keep it in my hands for him to take of whenever he delighted in doing so. Could he not see all the inner cuts he left me subject to? Did he care? What I was most afraid of was that although I was taking everything into account, I was still completely in love with him. It was like my mind was having a fistfight with my heart, but they both were losing. The next day he called but I didn't know what to say or how to feel. I was trapped, broken, and lost.

I felt like I was breathing while dead. I had no one to express myself or how I was feeling on the inside. I didn't want to tell the girls, I couldn't tell my mom, and other relatives would have perhaps killed him. I was in a losing situation, but God had other plans.

CHAPTER NINE

No More Apologies

I was waiting for normalcy to hit but it never did. We were separated but we didn't break up with one another. I wanted to see him, but I no longer trusted him. Things were crazy. Almost every day he would call to break up with me and call back and ask for us to stay together. Meanwhile, I was splitting on the inside. Then more hurt came. People say there is a thin line between love and hate, I say that depends on the individual's tolerance, intent, and heart. P.J. gave me every reason to hate him, but I loved him and that feeling never gave in. It was like everything was hitting at the same time.

I wasn't in my medical program anymore, but that's a different story. I probably should have fought it, but I didn't. I was starting over and starting anew. Before getting into my medical program, I was just about two classes away from graduating with my associate degree in arts. So, the two and a half years I spent in the medical program trying to get my associate in science for medical laboratory technology delayed my graduation for the regular associate in arts degree. However, once I started taking regular courses and prerequisites for an associate degree, I was told that I only had two courses left, which was a huge relief.

On top of that, I had already started education courses so that I could become a teacher. I remember I was in one of my classes when I received a mean text message from P.J. "You used me, and you let your mother disrespect me".

"You are a big leech", he screamed. I said that's funny. "Sure, a girl gives her virginity, moves in with you, drives you all around town when you lose your license, is with you through thick and thin, and helps take care of you when you get sick; cooks, and the whole nine, but somehow she is a user". "That's funny" I repeated. "No what's funny is when I cheated on you with Paula, I slept with her three times not once and one of the times was while over the phone with you" replied P.J. These words served as a slit to the back. When we were best friends, we would fall asleep over the phone together.

I would put the phone on mute and when we wake up, I would take it off mute to say good morning. When we began dating, we followed up with that same thing, until we started living with one another. I was already broken, now it's like he was stepping on me. I thought to myself how much more and would there be anything left? When it happens will it show? Because I felt like I was dying but only God knew. Was all this pain possible? Days had passed, and he was still calling with foolishness and arguing with me. After a few days of ranting, things went completely silent. I received no calls or text messages. I called but did not receive a response.

I wanted to go over to see him, so I found a way to his house. Upon knocking on the door, P.J. came out and sat down on the steps in the back. "Hey, I understand right now we are not on the best of terms, but that does not change my..." Before I could finish, P.J. interrupted me. "I'm sorry, Jalaina, but the truth is I never really was in love with you. I'm in love with Bella and I still am. I just loved you, but I am not in love with you," he said. With every fiber of me wanting to pour down in tears, I told myself I would not give him the benefit of that any longer. It was official, I was completely undone.

Days had passed, and he was still calling with foolishness and arguing with me. After a few days of ranting, things went completely silent. I received no calls or text messages. I called but did not receive a response. I wanted to go over to see him, so I found a way to his house. Upon knocking on the door, P.J. came out and sat down on the steps in the back. "Hey, I understand right now we are not on the best of terms, but that does not change my..." Before I could finish, P.J. interrupted me. "I'm sorry, Jalaina, but the truth is I never really was in love with you. I'm in love with Bella and I still am.

I just loved you, but I am not in love with you," he said. With every fiber of me wanting to pour down in tears, I told myself I would not give him the benefit of that any longer. It was official, I was completely undone. Mustering the strength to talk without crying, I said, "If you want, I could call her, let her know how much you love her and maybe she will listen to me". "No Jalaina it's too late Bella will never take me back," he said. "Okay well goodnight, I will go home, I love you". It wasn't that I was stupid. It was the fact that although he hurt me deeply, I loved him enough to let him go and see him happy.

I wanted him to have and achieve the love that I had for him. It makes no sense to be the only one benefiting from love in the worst way. In other words, I had who I wanted, but he wasn't satisfied, so that would be the worst way. That very night I caught a ride home from a loved one. When I reached home, I lay down and cried until I couldn't feel a thing. I cried until the night lost the fight to sunrise. I mustered up the strength to get up, take a shower, and go to school, although I didn't want to. I didn't want to do anything quite frankly. P.J. called while. I was at school.

"We are over, I do not want to be with you Jalaina. No more break, we are over". This was the last straw for me. For the first time, he heard me say "You are right we are over. I am done". "Remember I told you that every time you called me during our break to end the relationship it hurt me deeply, I also let you know that the next time you did this, it would be your last. It is the last". "Goodbye P.J.". When I hung up the phone, I took the escape route. The next couple of days were crucial. I felt as if life was going on, but I was at a standstill. P.J. called and asked for us to be together.

I told him no. After a week or so I finally answered the phone. "Jalaina, I love you. If I propose to you again, would you say yes", he asked. "No, I'm done now," I responded. I loved him, but I had to let go. I loved him, but I had to try to exist until I could live again, feel again, breathe again. My mouth told him I was done, while my heart longed for him. That night, P.J. showed up at the house. He called me on my phone and asked me to come out. I didn't want any commotion, so I came outside to talk to him while keeping my distance. P.J. rolled down the windows in his brother's black car and started talking to me.

During our conversation, out of nowhere, I heard him ask to kiss me. "Can I kiss you; can you give me a kiss?" he pleaded. "No, I can't, I'm sorry." This was one of the hardest denials of my life, but if I kissed him, I would have given in. P.J. left the house, speeding off. I worried for him and his life, but I had to choose me this time. As I walked into the house, I remembered what a prophet who lived in Georgia had told me when P.J. and I had first gone on a break. "Jalaina, he will come back, and you two can get married, but when he comes back, you will not want him," said Mr. D.

I remember telling him that would not be the case because I was irrevocably in love with P.J. I found out that we were both correct. I was in love, no doubt, but I couldn't trust the man I loved anymore. After that night, I started receiving threats from P.J. Pictures would come to the phone of my house when I was away. P.J. would leave threatening text messages, saying that before he took his life, he would go into some schools and churches. I was frightened, and I believe his family was too. I received a call from Mr. Mason who stated that he knew P.J., and I were in love with one another.

Mr. Mason also wanted to know if I would reconcile with P.J. as he had never seen his son behave like this. I softly declined Mr. Mason's request. I never told P.J.'s parents about the dreadful night. For a while, P.J. was very irate. So, when he showed up at my church, I almost lost it. On one fine Sunday, my mom and second mom had come to church with me. It was so beautiful being there with them, the three of us. While in church, I remember the Lord saying that P.J. was going to come to the church. In great fear, I rushed outside to see if I was crazy or if the Lord was speaking to me, and sure enough, P.J. came pulling up in his brother's black car.

I didn't know what he was going to do, and I was scared because I never reported the threats. I never reported him because I didn't want anything on his record. I wanted him to live and live well. I went inside and sat next to my family. When he came inside, fear ran through my bones worse than diarrhea out of the body. Just seeing him made all the pain come rushing in like a breech in a dam. "Jalaina, are you okay?" Jalaina, you're shaking," said Raina. While my second mom questioned what was going on, my mother looked directly at P.J. He walked past our aisle and went to the front of the church, sat down for a few minutes, and then got back up to leave.

As he walked past the aisle and left out of the double white doors, I went forward, and Raina caught me. My second mom held me that day in the church and wouldn't let go. It's like she knew without knowing. After that day, my focus was solely on trying to live. For the next couple of weeks, I began fasting and went back to eating meat. I was no longer a vegetarian; I was no longer P.J.'s girl. I had let go of the one I loved dearly to try and find myself. It was almost like a rebirth. However, even in all the pain, the Lord started speaking to me. The Lord started comforting me. I was not alone. Day after day, the Lord started taking the pain.

I found myself falling completely into His hands while He lifted me up, showed me purpose, and changed me completely. This was a process. Mental abuse is a type of control that leaves a deep scar, from the way you eat to the way you see yourself. I learned how to live and how to forgive myself. This took years, but eventually, I got past the pain. I understood that a lot of it was my fault because a person can only do to you what you allow. I allowed this, so this was something that had to be worked on in me. The pain and forgiveness process had an expiration date.

I learned that pain and passion yield a product. That product introduced me to part of my purpose. "Abba will give you a reason to go on; He'll enlighten your path and make you strong. Find your light and coverage in Christ up above; He will lift you up with His Agape love."

CHAPTER TEN

Finding Light: my note to Women

From fasting and seeking the kingdom, God filled me up and breathed life into me. God is truly a restorer. Although I was disobedient, God's grace saved me. A lot of women get out of abusive relationships and not all of them are aware that they are rescued by Christ and purpose. A lot of survivors believe that they made it out of their circumstance only because of determination and will to live. For those individuals, I will not take your survival story from you, but my story was and is different. I acknowledged that my survival story is only by the grace of God.

God spoke to me, rescued me, delivered me, and then sustained me. I was broken but I found life. I was able to see God in the name of Jehovah Nissi (the Lord my banner). I could have been at a place of going to jail as an accomplice, pregnant, or worse maybe catching a disease or something. However, the Lord shielded me from all those things. I was pouring in love and filling up someone's cup who had a hole in theirs. Do I regret the experience? Absolutely not. I needed everything that I went through because I wouldn't be the person I am today and have the relationship with God that I have. I not only found light, but I found God's voice.

I wrote this story through my lens, but everyone has their perspective. P.J. has a side as well. Understand, I am in no way writing this story to bash anyone, but I am writing this to help someone else who may be going through the same or worse.

My final message in this writing is a few notes. Note #1 Yes, there are warning signs before destruction but sometimes not always. Sometimes everything is fine until you are completely submerged because life happens, and people change. However, even then, it's never too late to walk away from a situation.

Note#2 Walking away and staying away is very hard and painful, but learning to live again is more rewarding than before the brokenness. You will and can possess a new identity and leave out stronger. This will require work, but it is possible. Sometimes the things that are broken and then fixed are better after being fixed. More beautiful, more unique. In the case of an actual human being; stronger, and wiser. It's not what you go through, it's the lesson learned in it, the mountain claimed after, and the wisdom passed on to the next individual who needs it. Trust me, with scenarios such as this, choose yourself.

Note #3 Never stay in something because you feel as if you are the blame or out of guilt. Pray and by practical means try to make things work. However, if it's abuse, walk away. Unless God informs you to stay; fly, skate, run, or roll if you have to, but baby please leave. If it's physical abuse, get out while you still can. The person will either kill you or you will kill them. Don't let it reach that far. That should be the last marker you ever allow in a relationship. As a matter of fact, it's too expensive to allow for your life is priceless.

Note#4 There is life after circumstance. Honey you will love again, it is possible. There is someone out there that will love you, even though the hurt. Having your true-life partner to love you through hurt is not always fair, so try to work on yourself before allowing anyone to come through that door.

Not to mention, you will have a time of grieving. Give yourself time to heal and be easy on yourself. Everyone goes through it in life but in different walks.

Note# 4 Do not allow anyone to put a time on your healing process. However, after 5 to 7 years, do not cry about the same thing, because in the end, you will cry more for the time you lost versus what you escaped from. This is with any circumstance of loss. Everything has an expiration date, don't waste your time crying over expired milk that you cannot drink and can no longer nourish. Clean it up and move on.

Note#5 Life experiences of relationships start from the home. Everything is a ship. Be careful how you allow one person to treat you because this paves the direction of how others will. Notice patterns and nip the ones that are not beneficial. A lot of the time when P.J. would say mean things to me he would always follow that up with "Yes, but I don't treat you how your family treats you". I allowed abuse from the ones that I loved nearest to me, so I eventually allowed the abuse from the one I wished to share my life with. Patterns and cycles. You are a human being, not a circus clown, guinea pig, or hamster. Get off the wheel.

Note #6 Listen, it is always important to have a job and your own money. Rather you are a man or woman. However, if you are in a relationship and you are down in a season of financial drought, your partner should not consistently throw this in your face and mistreat you because of it. Especially if you are putting in effort. This is a clear red flag to exit the relationship. I don't care if you have nowhere to reside. Never allow someone to make you feel like less than you are.

Think about it, if you two get married and life happens, things will only get worse. Suppose you become disabled; will this be consistently thrown in your face? Think about this. Marriage is supposed to be for a lifetime, it's not car leasing. When you are in a relationship with someone, you two are to keep each other. The Bible says in Ecclesiastes 4:11 -12 "Again, if two lie together, then they have heat: but how can one be warm alone? And if one prevails against him, two shall withstand him. Think about this.

Note #7 This note is one of the most important notes because seven represents completion. My seventh note of wisdom would be to put God first and foremost. God is completion, he is your home. God will show you how to love yourself. Love your neighbor as you love yourself, to do this you have to know how to love yourself!! Fall in love with yourself, nourish yourself, and complete things for you and in you. Remember God first then you. Everyone else comes after the two.

CONCLUSION

Dear reader, women give birth across the world every day. There is no lack in that aspect. However, there will never exist another you. No one can ever recreate you, even in genetic cloning. Therefore, love yourself, see yourself, and pour into yourself. You are God's masterpiece. Treat yourself better than a collector treats fine porcelain. Never stay in dangerous and mean situation out of guilt or love. Don't allow foolishness in your life. If you are in any type of abusive relationship; rather it be a sistership, friendship, husband ship, job ship, or daughter/mothership; choose you and get out while you still can.

Remember if you are dead and gone, life and your partner's life will still go on. Do not leave this world prematurely, especially without fulfilling purpose. Not to mention, once you get out of a relationship such as this, the hardest thing is not the part of leaving. The hardest part is living in the afterwards. The afterwards entail heart break, your families' questions, feeling like other things could have been done, denial, wondering if it was your fault, feeling of inadequacy, grief, regret, the shame of allowing such treatment, and the feeling of wanting to give up on and in life.

All these things can come at once or out of order, there are no specifics, it just depends on the individual. However, I can stand and say that yes everything listed is painful, but you can and will get through it, as well as grow through it, but you must have "the will to live" more than anything else.

I don't just want to exist I want to live. One can stay in an abusive situation for years, and not get killed but never really exists. Don't stay for the fear of leaving, be more afraid of staying and loosing yourself. There is joy that will come in the morning, and you will come to the light. There will be one morning that you wake up and things are better. Each day after will get a little bit better. There is hope after pain and bitterness. Fight for joy, fight to love again. Don't lose years because of the experience. Everyone is not your failed relationship, and don't jump into anything to fast because of the years lost. Discern things out, protect your heart, protect your joy and newness. Most importantly live, forgive and forgive yourself. I love you.

ABOUT THE AUTHOR

My name is Jamarra Jalaina Mota. I am a multiracial American woman, born and raised in North Miami, Florida. I am a child of the Most High God, determined to walk into greatness. As a minister, educator, author, and illustrator, I aim to educate and empower individuals one lesson at a time. I am inspired to make a positive change in my community and my profession. Writing allows me to express myself more creatively.

**For Booking
Ordering Information**
Ms. Jamarra Mota
Mota.jamarra@yahoo.com
Available on Amazon

Publisher's Information
MPC Creative Publishing & Designs, LLC
mpccreativepublishing@gmail.com
Ph: 954-479-2563

Made in the USA
Columbia, SC
01 October 2024